Amplifying Activ.
Experiential Lear

This book provides proven practical strategies and approaches to help you run your existing learning activities in new and more effective ways. It shows how by using distinct and deliberate strategies, teachers and trainers can guide and maximise the learning and development that their activity provides.

The 37 ideas can all be used independently and are appropriate for children and young people of different ages and abilities, and can be used in many different environments including outside, inside, classrooms, sports pitches and wilderness, and more. Each strategy is presented on a double page spread with illustrations, and consists of:

▶ Issues this strategy will help address
▶ How to implement this strategy
▶ The strategy in action, with examples from a wide selection of educational fields
▶ How this strategy helps maximise learning
▶ Any pitfalls to be wary of
▶ Other similar strategies to consider

Aimed at teachers, outdoor and adventure instructors, sports coaches, drama and music teachers and science educators, this is valuable reading for all educators wanting to deliver exciting experiential learning activities.

Sam Moore, having spent twenty years in adventure education and personal development in corporate, educational and youth settings, specialises in helping people develop themselves through challenge.

Tim Hudson is a creative thinker who loves working with people. The programmes he designs and delivers always have one overarching theme: helping people become the very best versions of themselves.

"Many books on experiential learning are strongly theory-led, whereas the writers' approach here, informed by years of practice, is much more direct - so it's an intelligent 'how-to' book, useful for those engaged in the daily struggles of experiential learning. There aren't enough such books yet..."

Bill Krouwel, *Senior Lecturer at Trinity College, Carmarthen*

Amplifying Activities for Great Experiential Learning

37 Practical and Proven Strategies

Sam Moore and Tim Hudson

Routledge
Taylor & Francis Group

LONDON AND NEW YORK

Cover image: Tim Hudson

First published 2023
by Routledge
4 Park Square, Milton Park, Abingdon, Oxon OX14 4RN

and by Routledge
605 Third Avenue, New York, NY 10158

Routledge is an imprint of the Taylor & Francis Group, an informa business

British Library Cataloguing-in-Publication Data
A catalogue record for this book is available from the British Library

Library of Congress Cataloging-in-Publication Data
A catalog record has been requested for this book

ISBN: 978-1-032-11739-3 (hbk)
ISBN: 978-1-032-11740-9 (pbk)
ISBN: 978-1-003-22129-6 (ebk)

DOI: 10.4324/9781003221296

Typeset in Source Sans Pro
by SPi Technologies India Pvt Ltd (Straive)

Printed in the United Kingdom
by Henry Ling Limited

Contents

CONTENTS

Acknowledgements

Thank you to all the people who have worked with us during careers that have involved organising and running thousands of hours of learning activities. You have all helped shape our practice, and hence this book. If you know us, and see your name in the examples of the strategies in action, yes, that is you! Thanks for being a role model; we were thinking of you when we wrote it!

The following all provided valuable feedback on the manuscript at critical stages, which was often nice, sometimes harsh, but always helped steer our progress for which we are grateful: Simon Beames, Colin Beard, Andrew Chicken, Jocelyn D'Arcy, Harvey Downey, Kirsty Edison, Lee Fisher, Jo Fromant, David Girling, Roger Greenaway, Di & Mike Hudson, Bill Krouwel, Mark Leather, Lorna Robinson, Tom Sowerby and Neal Stephenson.

Additional thanks to Annamarie Kino, who took a chance on two first-time authors who found themselves writing a book much to their own surprise!

Final thanks to our long suffering families without whom the book would have been written much sooner. Bertie, Charlie, Katy, Finn, Hanna and Ruth, we love you all.

About the Authors

Sam Moore

Sam is truly passionate about helping people develop themselves and specialises in adventure education. Having worked with the corporate sector and now focussed in the educational sector, Sam has worked with people of all ages, challenging them to think differently.

He has designed and run programmes that over ten-thousand people have benefitted from and are truly memorable for their creativity and impact.

Sam presents and writes for conferences on adventure education, and brings academic rigour and clarity to every programme he is involved in, ensuring he can always tell you not only what people are doing, but why they are doing it.

Tim Hudson

Early school reports correctly predicted that Tim would be a creative thinker with some unique ideas! Whilst his parents had mixed feelings about these unconventional talents, they have ultimately led him to pursue a degree in Management with a focus on organisational psychology, people and performance, and an eclectic but very fulfilling career.

On the way, he has delivered adventure education on land and sea, coached international sports people and teams, supported leaders during a merger of an aviation company, and worked with teachers aspiring to middle and senior leadership roles. His work always has one stand-out theme—helping people become the very best version of themselves.

Introduction

What is this book?

People learn from their experiences. There is no doubt about that. But what they learn and how much they learn varies wildly. Some experiences are instant lessons, 'Aha!' moments that are never forgotten. Other experiences are slow burners, drip-feeding learning into our brains over weeks, months or even years.

There are plenty of books about running activities, reviewing experiences and managing learning, many of which contain the *right* way to do it, at least according to the authors.

This book is not an attempt at a grand unified theory of facilitation but a series of sketch notes, each independent of the others, which describe one way in which you can approach the running of a task.

It won't give you any new activities to run but does suggest *strategies* that might help you run your existing activities in new ways. By taking a distinct and deliberate strategy, you can guide and maximise the learning and development that your activity provides.

The strategies in this book can support you in framing, setting up, briefing, running and reviewing your activities, and you should consider their impact on all these areas.

What is this book not?

Although many of the strategies in this book have their basis in academic models, this book is not intended as a textbook. Instead, it is a field-guide of tested, trusted strategies to help you run learning activities; a how-to guide backed by practice and experience. It is aimed squarely at those who offer learning experiences to help maximise the development that participants get from taking part.

How to use this book

This book should give you ideas and some starting points to think about new ways to run your activities. Each idea can be used independently; some before you start running a task, some during and some after.

If you are a logical person, you might want to start at the beginning and try the first strategy that excites you. If, however, you are the sort of adventurous person who flicks through a book, and starts on a random page in the middle, go ahead! Both methods are equally valid.

Who is this book for?

Every day, scores of educators go to work in classrooms, in lecture halls, on sports fields, on expeditions, at summer camps, and in a hundred other settings providing exciting and engag-

ing activities and tasks. Their hope is that their participants will learn something, gain some knowledge, refine a skill or change their behaviour..

Almost none of these people would call themselves a 'facilitator of learning experiences', but that is what they are. If you work with people, help them do things, and want them to learn and develop through that process, the ideas outlined in this book should have value to you.

Conscious thought about how you are going to run your activity can radically alter the outcomes for your participants. Your strategy will define the 'feel' of the experience for them, and can guide them towards the most useful outcomes. Planning your strategy helps ensure that learning isn't just an accidental by-product from your activities.

Throughout the book, we have used a mixture of examples from many different environments—outside, indoors, classrooms, wilderness, and many others—but each strategy will work in (nearly) all of them.

'Successful' activities

In a busy environment, it is all too easy to define 'success' in terms of the quantity of activities completed or a level achieved, they are, after all, easy things to measure. While this may give you a convenient number, it is not necessarily a useful one. In most cases, the true 'success' of an activity is the learning from it—something much harder to quantify.

If we worry less about the 'success' or 'failure' of a group to complete the task, we can focus more on the learning achieved through it. After all, there can often be more learning in failure than success.

Many activities can be used to provide a range of learning. Depending on how they are run and the language used to introduce and manage them, the same activity can introduce knowledge, develop skills or alter behaviour.

Understanding what it is you are trying to achieve allows you to make a conscious choice of strategy to maximise your chance of doing so.

Language and definitions

As much as possible, the language used in this book is that which you might use with your participants. Indeed, the word *participants* has been used widely, but this term could be replaced with students, delegates, members, clients, pupils or colleagues, as appropriate to the situation.

The words *task, challenge, activity* and *exercise* are used interchangeably, all meaning simply something that your participants will be doing.

Similarly, all the strategies are described as if you are working with groups, as this is more common, but virtually all are just as applicable to working in a one-to-one situation.

Choosing the Right Strategy

Many activities can be used to provide a range of learning, depending on how they are run and the language used to introduce and manage them.

A short expedition could be used to teach navigation skills and camp craft, or teamwork and resilience, or to provide an experience for participants to reflect upon and draw their own learning. All three are valid strategies, as is a combination of all three.

Choosing the right strategy is more art than science. There are no 'right' or 'wrong' strategies, only that which works and that which doesn't in a given situation.

Some of the strategies may seem similar at first glance, but they have subtle differences in their focus that will change the experience participants will have. For example, an activity made harder with the participants' knowledge (*Shifting Sands*) will feel different to them and have different outcomes than if you do it without them realising (*Pulling Strings*).

DOI: 10.4324/9781003221296-2

Strategies that take a similar approach to an issue are noted under the heading 'If you are looking at this you might like to consider…'.

Factors that affect the strategy you choose

Whether a strategy works might depend on lots of factors; the makeup of the group, activity, weather, how you are feeling, how the group are feeling, what worked last time, and what was for lunch. It is certainly not the case that what worked for one group or one activity last time will be guaranteed to work this time.

One of the skills that people who provide activities have to develop is the ability to consider all these factors, and any others that they think are important, and to select a strategy that provides the greatest benefits to their group.

The most effective way to develop this skill is to be thoughtful in choosing your strategy, and to experiment as much as possible. This book can help with both. It is true that you will make mistakes and have challenging sessions, but over time, you will develop a 'feel' for which strategy works when.

Some factors to consider

Learning outcomes

The most obvious factor, and the premise of the book, is that you should choose a strategy that matches the learning outcomes you want your participants to achieve. This is likely the first component you will think about, and each strategy has suggestions from the authors under the heading of 'Use this strategy to…'.

This is a particularly important factor to think about if your learning outcomes are not directly related to the activity, for example, if you are using practical tasks to build confidence.

Some useful questions to ask yourself when thinking about learning outcomes:

▶ Is it important that my group 'succeeds' or completes the task?
▶ Do my participants have a fixed learning outcome or is there flexibility to change?
▶ Do I want my participants to be challenged to help develop their competence or allowed an 'easy win' to develop their confidence?
▶ Do I want my participants to have lots of freedom or limited freedom?

Participants

Participants come in all shapes and sizes! A strategy that works for one group might not work for another group, even if they are superficially similar.

The age of your participants will significantly affect which strategy you choose. However, this is more related to maturity than calendar age; adult groups can show some amazingly childish behaviour at times, especially when under stress!

The number of participants you are working with will also strongly influence your choice of strategy. Some strategies work better with large groups, and some when the participants can be well supervised in small numbers.

Some other factors that might affect your choice of strategy include physical fitness, cultural background, gender, emotional state, previous experiences and any training they have received.

Some useful questions to ask yourself about your participants:

▶ How confident am I in my group's ability to undertake this activity?
▶ Do I think my group will need lots of help with this activity?
▶ Do my participants have the skills within the group to undertake this activity using this strategy?
▶ Are my participants ready for this activity?

Activity

The nature of your activity will be the third major factor affecting your choice of strategy. You will instinctively know that certain strategies are inappropriate for your chosen activity, but don't be afraid to experiment if you can do so safely. Using what appears to be an unconventional strategy with your activity can pay dividends, and your participants may surprise you.

If you have found a strategy that matches your learning outcomes well but are worried that it may not be suitable for your activity, it is worth thinking about how you may be able to adapt your activity to accommodate the strategy. This might mean simplifying it, reducing the risk, increasing supervision, providing more or different information, or altering the resources used.

Some useful questions to ask yourself about your activity:

▶ What strategies definitely won't work with this activity?
▶ Do I have sufficient resources to use this strategy with this activity?
▶ Can I adapt the activity to work better with my chosen strategy?
▶ How much time do I have?

Emotions

The emotional state of your participants can have a dramatic effect on the way in which activities run. As such, it needs to guide your choice of strategy.

The changing emotional state of participants is the primary reason that a strategy that worked well with a group, might not work well again with the same group, even if the activity and other factors are the same.

Their emotional state will be affected by many factors, but some to consider are:

▶ Recent success or failure
▶ Physical state, hunger, thirst, tiredness, etc.
▶ Stress level
▶ Relationships between team members
▶ Your relationship with them
▶ Previous experiences, both theirs and yours!

The emotional state of a group is a very dynamic factor, and one that takes skill and practice to assess. As such, your approach to choosing a strategy needs to be equally dynamic. However, if you are changing your strategy because a group's emotional state has changed, make sure it is a conscious choice, not an instinctive reaction or drift.

Some useful questions to ask yourself about your participants' emotional state:

▶ What are the consequences of my group performing poorly on this activity?
▶ Are my participants ready for this activity?
▶ How much emotional support will my participants need during and after this activity?

Risk

The physical safety of your participants should be paramount when running activities, and this is no less true when you are choosing a strategy to use. You should know the environments you are operating in and the tools you are using well enough to make informed decisions about the effect that a chosen strategy will have on the level of risk.

Physical safety is not the only form of risk; you should also consider the effect of your choice of strategy on the emotional, financial, reputational and environmental risks involved.

Some useful questions to ask yourself:

▶ Am I happy using this strategy with this activity?
▶ …with this group?
▶ …in this environment?
▶ …with assistance this far away?

If the answer is not a clear 'Yes' for all of them, reconsider your choices.

Context

Learning activities rarely happen in a vacuum. What happened before your activity, what is happening after, what happened last time your participants tried it, the time of day, how good lunch was and what the weather is doing might all affect your choice of strategy.

The context in which your activity is taking place is a key factor when choosing your strategy and is closely linked to the emotional state of the group.

How well you understand the context will depend on how long you have been with your participants and how much information you have, but it never hurts to talk to them to find out more.

If your activity is taking place as part of a wider set of activities, the timing of your activity in that series, the nature of previous activities and what is coming next will also impact your choices.

Some useful questions to ask yourself about the context:

▶ What have my participants been up to before they got to me?
▶ What will they be up to next?
▶ In what state do they need to leave this activity?

Combining strategies

There is also no need to limit yourself to only one strategy per activity.

You may choose to use one strategy while explaining what participants need to do, another while running the activity and a third while helping them to reflect. Combining strategies can be very powerful, but take care, lest the power of one strategy is reduced by introducing another. Again, with time, you will develop a 'feel' for which will work together and which don't.

Do not be afraid to switch strategies mid-activity if you think the group will benefit from it. Sagging morale may require you to change your approach from a *Questioner* to a *Cheerleader*, or a weak plan from the group may require you to be more hands on than you had hoped. It is also possible that your group would benefit from focusing on different learning outcomes, and that might prompt a change of strategy from you.

The important thing is to think consciously about the change you are going to make, rather than just let your strategy drift.

Strategies for common issues

Sometimes you know the issues that your participants are facing before you undertake an activity with them. Below are some suggested strategies to use to help you address some common issues that you and your participants may face.

If you want to...

...brief your participants differently

Consider using *Delegate, In the Picture, Listen Very Carefully, Mime Artist, Mysterious Voice, The Bigger Picture* or *Written Brief.*

...build participants' confidence

Consider using *Charge, Cheerleader, Devil on the Shoulder, Islands of Safety, Leg Up, Peer Expert, Pulling Strings, Train Tracks* or *Wind Up and Let Go.*

...challenge your participants

Consider using *Devil on the Shoulder, Devil's Advocate, Drag and Drop, Islands of Safety, Mime Artist, Pulling Strings, Questioner* or *Shifting Sands.*

...make it likely your participants will succeed

Consider using *Charge, Cheerleader, Iterative Goals, Leg Up, Saviour, Shifting Sands* or *Train Tracks.*

...empower your participants

Consider using *Abandon, Delegate, Free Rein, How High, Islands of Safety, Mysterious Voice, Secret Agent* or *Written Brief.*

...inspire your participants

Consider using *Saviour* or *Wizard.*

...motivate your participants

Consider using *Charge, Cheerleader, How High, Iterative Goals, Pulling Strings, Shifting Sands, Storyteller, The Bigger Picture* or *Wind Up and Let Go.*

...help your participants plan and organise

Consider using *Drag and Drop, Instruction Manual, Sum of the Whole* or *The Bigger Picture.*

...have your participants play and experiment

Consider using *Abandon, Free Rein, Islands of Safety* or *Playtime.*

...encourage your participants to reflect and review well

Consider using, *Fish Bowl, Instruction Manual, Plot Spoiler* or *Souvenir*.

...help your participants see the big picture

Consider using *Delegate, Fish Bowl, Hidden Agendas, Instruction Manual, Plot Spoiler, Sum of the Whole, The Bigger Picture* or *Wizard*.

...get your participants setting goals

Consider using *How High, Iterative Goals* or *Playtime*

...encourage your participants to solve problems

Consider using *Abandon, Drag and Drop, Free Rein, Help for Sale, Lifelines, Playtime, Questioner* or *Storyteller*

...ensure your participants support each other

Consider using *Fish Bowl, Listen Very Carefully, Peer Expert* or *Sum of the Whole*

...make your participants think about each other and their differences

Consider using *Delegate, Fish Bowl, Hidden Agendas, Peer Expert, Secret Agent* or *Sum of the Whole*

...get your participants to think for themselves

Consider using *Abandon, Devil on the Shoulder, Devil's Advocate, Hidden Agendas, In the Picture, Listen Very Carefully, Mime Artist* or *Written Brief*

...encourage your participants to use questions well

Consider using *Devil's Advocate, Help for Sale, Lifelines* or *Questioner*

Name	Reflect and review well	Think about others and differences	See the bigger picture	Support each other	Solve problems	Challenge	Using questions
Abandon					●		
Charge							
Cheerleader							
Delegate		●	●				
Devil on the Shoulder						●	
Devil's Advocate						●	●
Dtrag and Drop					●	●	
Fish Bowl	●	●	●	●			
Free Rein					●		
Help for Sale					●		●
Hidden Agendas		●	●				
How High							
In the Picture							
Instruction Manual	●		●				
Islands of Safety						●	
Iterative Goals							
Leg Up							
Lifelines					●		●
Listen Very Carefully				●			
Mime Artist						●	
Mysterious Voice							
Peer Expert		●		●			
Playtime					●		
Plot Spoiler	●		●				
Pulling Strings						●	
Questioner					●	●	●
Saviour							
Secret Agent		●					
Shifting Sands						●	
Souvenir	●						
Storyteller					●		
Sum of the Whole		●	●	●			
The Bigger Picture			●				
Train Tracks							
Wind Up and Let Go							
Wizard			●				
Written Brief							

Motivate	Drive to success	Inspire	Build confidence	Empower	Play and experiment	Think for themselves	Plan and organise	Set goals	Brief differently
				●	●	●			
●	●		●						
●	●		●						
				●					●
			●			●			
						●			
							●		
				●	●				
						●			
●				●				●	
						●			●
							●		
			●	●	●				
●	●							●	
	●		●						
						●			●
						●			●
				●					●
			●						
					●			●	
●			●						
	●	●							
				●					
●	●								
●									
							●		
●							●		●
	●		●						
●			●						
		●							
				●		●			●

The Strategies

Abandon

Give the group their instructions and play no further part

Use this strategy to...

Empower Your Participants	Encourage Your Participants to Solve Problems	Get Your Participants to Think for Themselves	Have Your Participants Play and Experiment

Sometimes the best strategy for helping your students to learn is to leave them to it. *Abandon* is a strategy where you set up the task or activity and explain it to your participants, before walking away and letting them get on with it completely. The planning of and method by which they tackle the task is left entirely in their hands.

This may mean literally walking away and not being present as the task is completed, or it may mean being physically present, but not interacting with the participants at all.

By giving complete ownership of the activity to your participants, you are allowing them to manage themselves and to fail or succeed entirely on their own ability and behaviour. This can be very empowering for them. To feel 'we did this ourselves' and to feel trusted to 'get on with things' helps build a sense of freedom, capability and independence.

Care must be taken in using *Abandon*; it isn't suitable for every activity. Giving your participants complete freedom means that their approach might be nothing like you envisaged, for better or worse. To be successful, you need to be clear in your objective, so your group has a definite goal to aim for.

The group must also be mature and skilled enough to attempt the task. They do not have to succeed, but you must not set them up to fail. If they do fail, it should be of their own making.

The safety of the participants must be considered when using *Abandon*. You must be sure that they are capable of dealing with any hazards that may be present without help or intervention from you.

The strategy in action

Kim is working with a group of students doing a media qualification. On a Friday evening, she sets them the challenge of creating a short film over a weekend.

She specifies it must be on the theme of 'The Future' and be seven minutes long. She gives them a line of dialogue, a prop, a character and a setting that must feature in their finished piece.

She shows them the equipment cupboard and the workspace they have and arranges to view their masterpiece at 5 p.m. on Sunday night. She leaves them with her phone number in case of emergencies and goes home.

As promised, she returns on Sunday evening, to watch whatever her students have produced, and to discuss the highs and lows of the production process.

DOI: 10.4324/9781003221296-4

How does this strategy maximise learning?

- ♀ *Abandon* forces the group to engage from the start, as they know that there will be no support from you later on.
- ♀ The group feels a real sense of ownership of the activity and the freedom to tackle it 'their way'.
- ♀ Participants are required to solve their problems within the team rather than take the easy option of asking for help.
- ♀ If a group succeeds, they should feel particularly proud of themselves as they have done so with no external help.

Pitfalls

- ⚠ *Abandon* is not suitable for tasks where safety would be a concern.
- ⚠ If you leave completely, you don't get to see and hear the group in action, and therefore can't add any observations into a review. If you don't 'leave' but are hanging about in the background, the group might not experience a complete sense of freedom.
- ⚠ You are unable to rescue a situation that has gone in a totally different, and perhaps undesirable, direction from any that you anticipated.
- ⚠ *Abandon* is a risky choice if you require the activity to be completed before being able to move on!

If you are looking at this you might like to consider...

- 🔍 Drag and Drop
- 🔍 Free Rein
- 🔍 Islands of Safety
- 🔍 Playtime

Charge

Go flat out, giving the group all the help they need to succeed and don't let their feet hit the ground

Use this strategy to...

Motivate Your Participants	Make It Likely Your Participants Will Succeed	Build Participants' Confidence

Sometimes it is really important for your participants to achieve their goal. This might be because they need a boost to their morale, because further parts of your activity rely on it, or that there are pressing safety concerns.

On these occasions, you can lead a *Charge* towards that goal, providing not only the direction but all the support the group needs to achieve it. That support might be in the form of encouragement, it might be advice or hints, it might be additional resources such as equipment or money, or it might involve getting 'hands on' with the task.

Charge is not about making the activity easier, but about driving your group towards their goal and ensuring they have everything they need to succeed. Their progress should feel high-paced and they should feel that success is inevitable if they work for it.

In using *Charge* you may well lessen both the feeling of success for the participants and potentially the learning they get from the activity. For this reason it should be restricted to situations where you feel the benefits of achieving their goal outweigh these disadvantages. This is a careful balancing act. In the worst case, you diminish the experience and you leave the group with reduced confidence, feeling like they wouldn't have succeeded without your help. In the best case, the group leaves the activity with increased confidence from their success.

Your role is to drive the pace and provide all the resources needed to ensure your group doesn't slow down or stop until they have completed the activity.

The strategy in action

As part of a Discover Science day at a local secondary school, Di is helping a group of students design and build cars powered by model rocket motors. Mindful that the highpoint of the day is racing the cars against each other down the track, she monitors their progress carefully.

She notices that one of the groups is struggling to get their prototype to work, are losing motivation, and are becoming disengaged. The day is halfway through, and it is obvious that their car won't make it to the start on time. They have also damaged some of their materials.

Di sits at their table, begins to help them get their design back on track, and replaces the materials that have been damaged. As she is doing this, she bubbles with enthusiasm for both the task and their attempt at it, encouraging them to take pride in their now functioning vehicle.

After a flurry of activity, the team made it to the start line of the race, and though they didn't win, they came away inspired by the event and the science they have accessed.

DOI: 10.4324/9781003221296-5

How does this strategy maximise learning?

- 💡 By virtually ensuring success, you can boost the participants' morale and confidence.
- 💡 Your group feels supported and doesn't have any time to get nervous, or for the nerves from one person to spread to the group.
- 💡 This can be useful if you are aware the group isn't that keen on your activity or are reluctant to take part.
- 💡 If you are short of time, for example, if the environmental conditions or timetable is changing, *Charge* lets you drive the pace.

Pitfalls

- ⚠ By taking away some of the group's independence, you run the risk that their feeling of success is reduced.
- ⚠ If you *Charge* too hard, you can either leave the group behind, figuratively or literally, or you can create a sense of panic within the group.
- ⚠ There is a risk that the group ends up 'doing' and not 'thinking', which reduces the opportunity for them to learn the broader lessons from the activity.

If you are looking at this you might like to consider...

- 🔭 Cheerleader
- 🔭 Train Tracks
- 🔭 Wind Up and Let Go

Cheerleader

Provide constant praise and enthusiasm to propel your group
to success

Use this strategy to...

Motivate Your Participants	Make It Likely Your Participants Will Succeed	Build Participants' Confidence

Barely a single sports match takes place in the USA without the presence of a troupe of brightly clad gymnasts and dancers performing routines, singing loudly and adding loads of energy to both the crowd and the players. Sometimes what your participants need is an overwhelmingly positive, excited, enthusiastic, dynamic *Cheerleader* to spur them on in their task.

This is normally when a team has all the skills they need for a task, but it is still daunting to them, perhaps because it will be arduous, long or they lack belief in their abilities. On these occasions, you can be their *Cheerleader*.

Here you take the responsibility of putting in the energy into the group. Your role is to constantly find ways to praise the members of the team. This could be praise for positive behaviours (such as being supportive or logical) or actions (such as correctly finding a piece of the answer).

Instead of offering advice or guidance on how the team should proceed, your role is to exude total confidence in them, providing cheerful, enthusiastic motivation and never allowing them to doubt for a moment that you believe they can complete their task. Repeatedly asserting your belief in them, helping them see how much they have already achieved, putting the challenges ahead in perspective, praising both effort and achievement, individually and together, you are a rock of positivity they can look to when they don't feel these things themselves.

By adding as much positive energy as possible to the proceedings, you help the group to believe in themselves. After all, how can anyone so confident and enthusiastic be wrong?

The strategy in action

Zoë has taken her group on a canoe trip. They have spent the morning paddling the length of a long lake and taken a break for lunch on the beach at the far end. The weather has been cold, sunny and still all morning, but over lunch the wind picks up, blowing down the lake, and they will be paddling into it all the way back to the jetty where they started.

Having seen the group paddle all morning, Zoë knows they have the skills and are strong enough to get back, but she also knows it will be a long slog. As they begin packing up the food, she transforms herself into a cheerleader, acknowledging the challenge ahead but praising the team for their earlier paddling. As they launch and set off into the wind, she remains relentlessly cheerful and, even when the participants find the going tough, she remains confident in their abilities and enthusiastic about their progress, and her enthusiasm rubs off on them.

DOI: 10.4324/9781003221296-6

How does this strategy maximise learning?

- ♀ *Cheerleader* is helpful if your group lacks belief in themselves.
- ♀ You are hands on and can strongly steer your group to success, although that doesn't mean you have to give all the answers!
- ♀ Your positivity will transfer to the group, and they should leave with lots of energy and feeling good about themselves.

Pitfalls

- ⚠ It is harder to have 'tricky' conversations from a position of *Cheerleader*. Should you need to do this, it can be hard to re-establish your role as the *Cheerleader*.
- ⚠ You are a very present part of their exercise, and therefore can end up as a safety net that the group relies on and becomes complacent about having.
- ⚠ Being a *Cheerleader* is very hard work and can leave you exhausted if it goes on too long!

If you are looking at this you might like to consider...

- 🔭 Charge
- 🔭 Leg Up
- 🔭 Wind Up and Let Go

Delegate

Give someone in the group part or all of your job

Use this strategy to...

Empower Your Participants	Brief Your Participants Differently	Make Your Participants Think about Each Other and Their Differences	Help Your Participants See the Big Picture

Delegating is the skill of passing over some or all of your responsibilities and duties to someone else. It can be a very powerful tool for developing your participants if used properly.

Where your activity has specific roles or sections, these can be parcelled out to group members, allowing them to feel responsible and engaged in what they are doing. Choosing the right person for the right role is a subtle art, but done well can raise both attainment and a participant's sense of achievement.

This strategy is powerful both when allowing participants to excel in a role they will be good at and when they are challenged by a role they naturally find hard. You can also use it to highlight the strengths of a participant, and with care, their weaknesses too.

A nice way to start delegating is to think about the components of your role as a teacher, coach or instructor and to see if you can give some of these components to the group to do. For example, you could hand over some or all of the briefing of a group, the planning of the activity, the policing of any rules, or the review at the end.

You can control the scale of thinking a participant has to do by delegating carefully. A delegated leader might have to raise their viewpoint to consider the whole task ahead, whereas someone who has a delegated minor role is 'given permission' to forget the big picture and to excel in that small area.

This strategy is also great for starting to develop leaders within the group. The simple task of asking someone to introduce and explain the activity will often have the knock-on effect that questions will be directed to them, as opposed to you. Through this, they become an informal leader, and with support they can continue in this role.

The strategy in action

Kay works with a youth theatre group who are putting on a performance of *Fiddler on the Roof*. At the planning meeting she is choosing who will take on which roles.

One participant is confident and has been involved in plays before, but has never been a stage manager, so she offers her that role as a challenge.

Another participant is keen to be involved but nervous, and Kay thinks he has potential, so she offers him the role of prop management, which will allow him to focus on that area alone.

A third participant is at the theatre group because her parents want her to be, and she seems disengaged with the activity. Kay suggests she might like to operate the sounds and effects, at which the participant perks up.

A fourth member of the group is very confident, but Kay suspects he hasn't quite as much experience as he is suggesting. She lets him head up to the lighting booth, and watches his face fall when he realises how complicated it is. She asks him to be in charge of lighting anyway, but stands ready to support him if needed.

DOI: 10.4324/9781003221296-7

How does this strategy maximise learning?

- ♀ *Delegate* empowers both the individuals and the group to feel like they are in control of the activity.
- ♀ Used well it can provide differentiation in the development of different members of the group. In particular, *Delegate* can be used to stretch participants who are finding the activity easy.
- ♀ *Delegate* can be used to draw a disengaged member of a team back into the activity, by ensuring they have a specific role to play.
- ♀ By passing on some of your responsibilities, *Delegate* reduces your workload, which allows you to focus on ensuring that the desired learning is happening.

Pitfalls

- ⚠ By handing some of the responsibilities to members of the group, you lose some control of the activity and its outcome, which might have an impact on timetables, safety, desired learning or morale.
- ⚠ Delegating the wrong role to someone can damage their confidence or show up their weaknesses in an uncontrolled way.
- ⚠ Once you hand over responsibility for a task or area, if you need to take it back, you risk undermining the confidence and authority of the participant you gave it to.

If you are looking at this you might like to consider...

- 🔍 Hidden Agendas
- 🔍 Peer Expert
- 🔍 Secret Agent
- 🔍 Written Brief

Devil on the Shoulder

Consciously provide unhelpful comments and bad advice to provide a challenging environment

Use this strategy to...

Get Your Participants to Think for Themselves	Challenge Your Participants	Build Participants' Confidence

Sometimes it can be valuable to create a 'hostile' environment for your participants to operate in. This should be done consciously and carefully, and with a group with whom you have a high level of trust.

At one extreme, you can openly and actively criticise and disparage participants' progress, providing negativity and questioning everything they do. At the other end of the spectrum, you can quietly and subtly sow seeds of doubt in their minds that they are doing the right thing.

In both cases, the aim is to help your participants develop a defiant, inner confidence that will carry them through difficulties when the environment around them gets tough. They should be developing a psychological strength and a 'we are going to do this, despite what the naysayers think' attitude.

This is a particularly useful strategy if your group have become reliant on you for external reassurance about their abilities. It should be used very carefully as it can quickly make you unpopular and damage the group's trust in you.

This strategy is a bit like a power tool, used skilfully it can be very effective, but it has the potential to do a lot of damage very quickly to the relationship between you and your group!

The strategy in action

Anita is overseeing a four-day back-packing expedition in the mountains of Wales. It is the third day and the weather has been variable, with a mix of sun and rain. The participants are a capable group but are low in spirits, and at a rest break are whining about their situation.

Anita considers the group carefully, and then offers them the chance to walk home. She points out a short cut back to their vehicles and suggests that if they don't want to finish the expedition they should take it. She says she is sad that they won't achieve their goal, but she understands if they feel they aren't up to it.

A defiant mood takes over the group and they reject her offer, they set off on the next leg with a new determination and are proud that they didn't take the easy option. Anita reverts to her usual supportive self and sets about ensuring that her relationship with her team wasn't too damaged by her strategic negativity.

DOI: 10.4324/9781003221296-8

How does this strategy maximise learning?

- 💡 The reverse psychology involved in *Devil on the Shoulder* is great for developing independence and defiant confidence.
- 💡 Disparate groups start to come together when given a 'common enemy'.
- 💡 It is a useful metaphor for many real-world situations where participants might encounter hostility or indifference.

Pitfalls

- ⚠ This is a strategy that comes with significant risk of damaging or destroying your relationship with your participants.
- ⚠ It can be difficult to make this strategy feel authentic, if normally you have a supportive relationship with the group and you suddenly change your approach.
- ⚠ A group or participant's confidence can easily be damaged by the negativity of this strategy.
- ⚠ There is the potential for a knock on consequence for future activities if the group start to think they have reason to be sceptical of any advice you give.

If you are looking at this you might like to consider...

- 🔍 Devil's Advocate
- 🔍 Questioner

Devil's Advocate

Always offer alternative viewpoints to those offered by group members

Use this strategy to...

Get Your Participants to Think for Themselves	Challenge Your Participants	Encourage Your Participants to Use Questions Well

The *Devil's Advocate* is someone who always offers the opposite opinion. You can take on this role by constantly offering alternative viewpoints to any that the group put forward.

Used carefully, this can be a valuable way of challenging your participants, sowing doubt and causing them to second guess any decisions they are making, which helps them be more certain of their decisions once made. When they create ideas in an environment where you are always offering alternatives, the participants are likely to consider a wider range of options. In addition, the option they finally choose will have been robustly tested and they should feel more confident in it.

The point isn't to directly challenge the ideas a participant is putting forward, or to tell them they are wrong, but to constantly and subtly provide other ideas to broaden their thinking and help them ask themselves the right questions. It is often more powerful to phrase your alternative viewpoint as a question such as 'Have you thought about…?' to avoid conflict and to encourage them to ask their own questions.

This strategy only works when there is a good level of trust between you and your group. If used carelessly, it is easy to become annoying or appear negative. Having their ideas constantly challenged can quickly demoralise a group, or cause internal conflict between participants.

Alternatively, in an ideal world, the group will take on the role of *Devil's Advocate* themselves, either formally or informally, to help strengthen their decision making.

The strategy in action

Jenny has just been assigned the role of a mentor to a new apprentice who has arrived at her workplace. She is responsible for some of their professional development.

The new employee is confident and keen, and Jenny feels that they are making quick decisions without taking into account wider issues facing their company, and this has started to produce some friction with other employees.

She arranges a conversation with the apprentice to discuss their progress, and casually and in a supportive manner begins to play *Devil's Advocate* to their proposed ideas. Whenever they put forward an idea, Jenny counters it with an alternative or presents a problem with it. By suggesting other courses of action and asking challenging questions, she hopes to broaden the new employee's view and get them to think more deeply about the decisions they make.

Although the apprentice initially finds Jenny's approach challenging, they gradually come to realise that through using it, she has helped them produce ideas that are better received.

DOI: 10.4324/9781003221296-9

How does this strategy maximise learning?

- *Devil's Advocate* is a good way to get a group really confident in their plan, as you have 'helped' them think more deeply about a wider range of options.
- This strategy encourages the use of questions as a tool in decision making.
- Handled well, *Devil's Advocate* can be used to steer participants away from poor decisions and towards better ones, without removing their authority to make the decision.
- With a mature group you can delegate the role of *Devil's Advocate* to a participant.

Pitfalls

- It is very easy to demoralise or frustrate participants if they are constantly being questioned.
- You can easily damage your relationship with your participants by being a *Devil's Advocate*, and they can start to see you as the 'enemy'.
- A less confident group may well feel they need your approval for their ideas and may struggle if they are not given it.
- Inevitably your activity will slow down, as you don't let quick decisions happen.

If you are looking at this you might like to consider...

- Devil on the Shoulder
- Questioner

Drag and Drop

Support the group in their planning and leave them alone during the task

Use this strategy to...

Challenge Your Participants	Encourage Your Participants to Solve Problems	Help Your Participants Plan and Organise

In this strategy, you help the participants as much as possible to create an excellent plan that is likely to succeed, then step back and let them carry out that plan with the minimum of interference from you.

Some activities require participants to spend a substantial amount of time planning their actions before they start, in some cases the planning may even take longer than the task. This is particularly true of high risk activities or those for which they will only have one attempt.

The *Drag and Drop* strategy is to make yourself a part of the participants' planning process, helping them with their research, managing discussions and steering them towards ideas that are likely to be successful. You don't create the plan for them, but you are heavily involved. By the end of this phase, you should be confident that they have created a really solid, detailed, realistic plan that is likely to be successful.

At this point you step back, let the participants start the activity and carry out their plan on their own, only stepping in if they are engaging in risky behaviour. As much as possible you should be entirely hands-off. Even if the plan begins to fail, or they begin to deviate from it, allow them to wholly own this phase of the task through any bumps and issues, all the way to 'success' or 'failure'.

The strategy in action

Becky is taking a school group on a two-day expedition in the Cairngorms. She provides her group with the start and finish locations, location of the campsite where they will sleep, the maps they need, and weather forecast. Working with them, she helps them develop a route, work out their times of departure and expected return, write a kit list, develop an emergency plan and assign roles to team members.

The next morning, they get out of the minibus at the trail, and after a few final words of advice, the group set off, with Becky walking with them, carrying out their plan with minimal intervention from her.

Without interference from her they arrive at the campsite that evening, and after a good meal, climb into their tents and sleep well. The next day Becky feels confident in their abilities, so after confirming their plan, she drops back and allows them to return unaccompanied to the minibus.

DOI: 10.4324/9781003221296-10

How does this strategy maximise learning?

- ♀ *Drag and Drop* creates a clear separation between planning and execution, which forces your participants to spend time creating a plan which they must all agree on.
- ♀ You have a high level of influence on the success of the task, as you remain 'active' in the group until they have a good plan that is likely to work.
- ♀ Your group will start the task confident as they know they have a good plan.
- ♀ If you have let your group carry out the task without interference, they will feel they have achieved success from their own efforts.

Pitfalls?

- ⚠ *Drag and Drop* is difficult to use in a high skill or high risk environment, when intervention from you is likely to be needed.
- ⚠ You run the risk of not letting the group be creative in their thinking if you end up steering their plan.
- ⚠ If you are a significant part of creating the plan, and it doesn't execute well, you run the risk of being 'blamed'— that sense of 'you gave us a plan that didn't work'.

If you are looking at this you might like to consider...

- 🔍 Abandon
- 🔍 Free Rein
- 🔍 Train Tracks
- 🔍 Wind Up and Let Go

Fish Bowl

Take a participant out of the activity and get them to observe what is going on

Use this strategy to...

Ensure Your Participants Support Each Other	Help Your Participants See the Big Picture	Make Your Participants Think about Each Other and Their Differences	Encourage Your Participants to Reflect and Review Well

When participants are engaged in an activity, they are often concentrating hard on the task in hand and they lose sight of the bigger picture. This picture might be of the overall progress of the task or it might be the interactions within the team.

By lifting a participant out of the activity and allowing them to observe rather than take part, we allow them to look into the *Fish Bowl* they have just come out of, which gives them the chance to gain valuable insights that might be lost while taking part. There is value for the participant, whether the focus of their observations is on getting better at the activity or studying the way a group operates in order to draw wider learning from the activity.

The exact format in which you do this is a matter of judgement. When you select a participant to 'come out of the *Fish Bowl*', you can either give them some suggestions on what to look for, or leave them to make their own. On some occasions it might be useful for them to later share their observations with the group, on others they might simply use them for their own development.

In general you don't want the participant to interact with the group while they are outside the *Fish Bowl* in order to give them time to just observe and to maintain their detachment from the detail of the activity. On longer tasks, you may like to set intervals after which they can interact with the group for a time, if it would be useful to provide them with feedback in a timely manner.

With younger, less mature or less skilled groups, you can sit with the person on the outside and share with them what you are noticing, to help them develop their observation skills.

The strategy in action

Hanna is running a day of training for her school's student leaders, which they refer to as 'prefects'. Over the day, the prefects work in small groups to complete a series of tasks, each of which demonstrates an aspect of leadership to them.

There are six prefects in each group and six tasks, so for each one, Hanna asks a different student to step back from the group and make notes on their communication, teamwork and problem-solving ability. After the task, that student is then given the chance to lead a review with their group and to discuss their thoughts.

By not getting involved in the detail of a task, the selected students have the opportunity to observe the interactions of the team, to understand how different people work and have a chance to practice giving feedback.

DOI: 10.4324/9781003221296-11

How does this strategy maximise learning?

- This strategy is very powerful for demonstrating the value in seeing the bigger picture.
- It can be used to give quieter people a role and a voice in the group conversation.
- Being out of the *Fish Bowl* allows participants to focus much more on the dynamics within a team without getting lost in the task.
- Feedback from peers can be much more accepted and powerful than that from teachers, coaches or instructors.

Pitfalls

- Removing one team member from an 'exciting' activity can cause resentment as they don't get to take part.
- Participants who are not used to observing can feel awkward 'spying' on their team or uncomfortable giving feedback afterwards.
- People behave differently when they know they are being observed, so the observer might not get a 'true' perspective on the team's dynamics.

If you are looking at this you might like to consider...

- Plot Spoiler
- Secret Agent

Free Rein

Tell the group the objective, then give them free rein to work out how they will achieve it

Use this strategy to...

Empower Your Participants	Encourage Your Participants to Solve Problems	Have Your Participants Play and Experiment

Sometimes you will be working in an environment where you can give your participants *Free Rein* to operate within parameters that you set. With this strategy you tell the group what it is that you want them to achieve, but leave them to worry about how to achieve it.

This is particularly powerful if you want them to take complete ownership of the task and to solve all the problems that come their way. This mirrors many real life situations where how something is achieved is often less important than the result.

You may wish to set rules or guidelines for their approach, but do this as lightly as possible, as the more constraints there are, the less *Free Rein* they have and the less effective this strategy will be. Rules might sensibly cover things like safety, legality, timescales or cost, which mirrors the real world.

Your description of what you want your team to achieve must be clear, accurate and precise, otherwise you might be very surprised what you end up with! It should be totally clear to everybody if the goal has been met. It is great to see the creativity this strategy allows and a participant's solution to the task can often be far better than any you had in mind.

A good guideline when explaining what you want your team to achieve is to ensure you cover the 'Who, What, When, Where and Why' and then you can leave them to think about the 'How'!

The strategy in action

To help his students think more creatively in design technology lessons, Finn decides to set them an open challenge. He places a basket hoop at one end of the workshop and sets them the goal of firing a tennis ball from on top of the front desk into the hoop.

He provides them with access to the material store, details of which tools they are allowed to use and two hours until they must demonstrate their creation. He reminds them to be safe and sensible, and that the usual workshop rules still apply and then steps back to let them get on with it.

After two hours the teams all have a device but the design varies hugely and includes at least one that Finn has never seen before. Some are more successful than others, but all the participants agree that being given *Free Rein* was not only fun but it also made them think much harder than usual.

DOI: 10.4324/9781003221296-12

How does this strategy maximise learning?

- By allowing your participants Free Rein, you encourage them to engage with the task and be as creative as possible.
- *Free Rein* mirrors much of what happens in the 'real world' where outcomes are more relevant than methods.
- The freedom and the process of doing all the thinking for themselves makes for an intense experience, which helps participants retain information and develop themselves.
- It is great fun watching participants exercise *Free Rein*, and you might learn something from their approaches!

Pitfalls

- Sometimes participants need a bit of guidance to get them going as they can find starting completely from scratch intimidating!
- The more rules or constraints you have to set for your activity, the less *Free Rein* the participants feel they have.
- Allowing your group true *Free Rein* can involve significant amounts of resources as restricting their resources too much can reduce their freedom to innovate.
- Some groups may misuse the freedom they have been given, and they can feel aggrieved if they perceive you are removing some of that freedom by stepping in.
- As with any strategy where you give participants freedom, you reduce the certainty of the outcome, and with *Free Rein* you lose control of the process as well!

If you are looking at this you might like to consider...

- Abandon
- Drag and Drop
- Playtime

Help for Sale

Give the group opportunities to buy help as needed

Use this strategy to...

| Encourage Your Participants to Use Questions Well | Encourage Your Participants to Solve Problems |

One way to encourage your participants to consider how often they ask for help is to run your activity in such a way that there are consequences for doing so. If a team has to trade resources they consider valuable in order to ask a question, they will hopefully think hard about what and when to ask before they do so.

The simplest version of *Help for Sale* is to give your participants fictional 'money' that they can then pay you to ask for information. When the money runs out, so does the help! The information doesn't have to be in the form of a question, it could be that you have prepared hints, clues, information sheets or that it gives them access to a certain number of minutes of conversation. Indeed, the help doesn't even have to be information, it might be more resources, more team members or even more time to complete the task.

Instead of fictional money, the group could also spend other resources, such as some of the materials for the task, points, and 'human' resources by putting a team member into a sin-bin. If your participants have a budget with real money to spend, they could use some of it to buy advice.

When realising help has consequences, participants are more likely to consider whether they really need it and are more likely to think through what they need before asking. This can help participants to think critically, to be more self-confident and to formulate good questions. This relates to the 'real world' where most help comes with a cost of some sort.

The strategy in action

Martin is a counsellor at a camp for teenagers and organises an activity where each team is asked to design a raft that they will use in a race later the same day. They are given £50 and told that in three hours' time they will be able to visit a local hardware store to buy the materials they need to build their raft.

Knowing that when they first start, his campers often struggle to generate realistic ideas for their rafts, Martin offers five minutes of advice sessions with him, but these will cost the teams £5 each session.

Two of the teams buy advice sessions after half an hour of planning. One arrives with a list of questions and quickly gathers all the information they need. The other arrives less prepared and is back half an hour later to buy a second session.

Both teams agree that the £5 was worth it, but they then had to be more careful with what they spent in the hardware store.

DOI: 10.4324/9781003221296-13

How does this strategy maximise learning?

- ♀ Knowing help comes at a cost will encourage the group to think about problems for themselves before they ask for it.
- ♀ It's easy to make any exercise easier and harder for different ability groups before you start by setting the 'price' of help lower or higher respectively.
- ♀ When asking for help incurs a cost, participants will often carefully phrase their questions or requests more carefully than without.
- ♀ *Help for Sale* is a good way to support multiple groups, as you can position yourself as a 'central help desk'.

Pitfalls

- ⚠ Participants can still get stuck on an activity if they spend all their 'money' and haven't got the answers to help them complete it.
- ⚠ Even if you have given them the exact assistance they asked for, if it doesn't help a group proceed, they might end up feeling animosity towards you.
- ⚠ Some participants might take the 'easy' route of buying help for a problem that they could solve without it, removing the opportunity for them to solve the problem for themselves.
- ⚠ It can be hard to generate real consequences for using resources, which can lead to *Help for Sale* feeling artificial.

If you are looking at this you might like to consider...

- 🔍 Leg Up
- 🔍 Lifelines

Hidden Agendas

Give each member of the group a hidden goal to achieve alongside the task

Use this strategy to...

Make Your Participants Think about Each Other and Their Differences	Help Your Participant See the Big Picture	Get Your Participants to Think for Themselves

In real life situations, it is not unusual for people working in the same team to have different goals. These may be overt, where others in the team are aware of them, or hidden. These individual goals may be close to the group's stated aim, or they may be hugely different. It is not necessarily a problem to have differing aims within a team, but it can lead to disagreements and conflict.

You can simulate and explore this situation during your activities by giving some or all of your participants *Hidden Agendas* that differ from or extend the challenge you have set the group. This might be achieving a certain score, using a specific technique, completing within a certain time or perhaps even to prevent the task from being completed.

Sometimes these *Hidden Agendas* will be broadly in line with the overall aim of the group, but with a mature set of participants, you can introduce wildly differing goals, competing goals or even create factions with a team. The way a team handles these situations can provide useful discussion during a review of the task.

You can assign these agendas such that the team knows they exist but not what they are, or you can assign them discreetly so that some people don't know that their teammates have differing goals.

The agendas could relate to the task in hand, for example, making sure they spend as little money as possible, or it could be related to the behaviour of the team, such as ensuring everyone is listened to.

As with all strategies that involve deception or withholding information, care must be taken to ensure that it is used positively and to gain the desired learning. Used badly it has the possibility to destroy trust within a team and between you and your participants.

The strategy in action

Brian is meeting with the student leaders at the school where he is a teacher. He has been asked to work with them to create designs for a new school logo.

The student leaders are a friendly group, and Brian is concerned that they aren't willing to challenge each other's ideas if they think it will cause upset. He decides to give each of them a *Hidden Agenda* to stimulate conversation and encourage debate. He quietly catches each student before the meeting and gives them an individual goal to complete alongside the main task of designing a logo.

The individual goals he gives are:

- The logo must use school colours and be vibrant.
- The logo must look good when photocopied in black and white.

DOI: 10.4324/9781003221296-14

- The logo must contain the school name.
- The logo must include an animal.
- The logo must be ready by the end of the meeting.
- They must produce four different logos to present to senior staff.

Over the course of the meeting, the students discuss and develop designs, each pushing for their *Hidden Agenda*. Not all the students manage to achieve their goal, but the designs produced are varied and interesting, and the conversation is lively and robust.

How does this strategy maximise learning?

- *Hidden Agendas* are extremely common in the 'real world', so practice dealing with them is useful.
- This strategy challenges teams to find solutions that solve a collection of goals, make them think more broadly and consider more options to find a 'win-win' outcome.
- In doing so, participants must listen to and understand others so they can understand their desires.
- Participants may also have to come to terms with the fact that they cannot all meet their goals, or that other people's goals may have to take precedence.

Pitfalls

- Given the secretive nature of *Hidden Agendas*, a group may turn against each other or against the person who set them up, damaging the trust.
- Some groups may feel they have been set up to fail if all members of the team can't achieve their own goals.
- It is easy for the main focus of the activity to be lost amongst everyone's personal agendas.
- Less confident members of a team might struggle to advance their own agenda in the face of louder team members, further damaging their confidence.

If you are looking at this you might like to consider...

- Secret Agent
- Sum of the Whole

How High?

Let the group set their own measure of success

Use this strategy to...

| Empower Your Participants | Get Your Participants Setting Goals | Motivate Your Participants |

Where a task has a clear, measurable outcome such as a time, distance or score, you can allow the participants to set their own goal and work towards achieving it. This allows them the experience of overcoming a challenge they have created themselves. Being able to set a goal that is challenging but achievable is not only exciting and motivating but a useful skill in its own right.

Perhaps the easiest way to do this is to guide the group through the task or challenge for the first time, so that they understand what is expected of them. Then let them have a go at setting a score, time, distance, etc.

You can then ask the group to improve on this benchmark and to set a new goal, a measurable improvement *they* want to make. This will allow them to problem-solve, practice, and find ways to improve, until they reach it. If time permits or they find it easy to reach their goal, they can then set themselves another goal to aim for, and so on.

Once time runs out, or if the mood of the group is appropriate, it can be motivational to compare the initial benchmark score with their final result to see how far they have come.

The strategy in action

Steve is working with a group of athletes who are competing in the 4 x 100m relay at an upcoming athletics meet. They are a new team, and he can see several places where refinements can be made, but, in the first instance, he decides to hand responsibility for improvement to the athletes themselves.

Once out on the track, he sets them up for a trial and they run the course in 50.1s. Gathering them together, he asks them to think about their performance, and where they could have improved it. After hearing a few ideas, he asks them to quantify how much those improvements are worth.

As a team, they decide that they can save at least 1.5 seconds, especially at the changeovers, and so set themselves a target of 48.6s and spend the rest of the session looking to make those improvements. After an hour they record a time of 48.5s and retire to the changing rooms proud, excited and motivated for the upcoming competition.

DOI: 10.4324/9781003221296-15

How does this strategy maximise learning?

- With careful use, *How High* provides your group with a sense of 'ownership' of the task, increasing participants' engagement with the objective.
- By letting your group set their own goals, your group is less likely to feel like they are 'doing it for the teacher' and more like they are doing it for themselves.
- If you encourage the group to think through the exercise first, they are more likely to consider what is realistically achievable before they start.
- You provide your group an opportunity to practice setting challenging but realistic goals.

Pitfalls

- Your group may need significant guidance to set goals that are both realistic and challenging, reducing the effectiveness of the strategy.
- Your participants could pick a goal that is easily achieved, and then your exercise might not fill up the time you had allotted and could leave them feeling underwhelmed.
- If your group sets their heights too high, they may disengage with the exercise when they realise their goal is unattainable, leaving you with a judgement to make about stepping in and supporting them to set an easier target, or letting them struggle on.
- If your group cannot agree on a goal, conflict can arise which might distract from the learning you intended for them.

If you are looking at this you might like to consider...

- Delegate
- Free Rein
- Iterative Goals

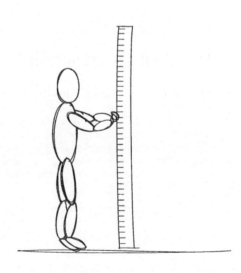

In the Picture

Hand the group picture instructions with all the information they'll need and leave the participants to follow them

Use this strategy to...

Brief Your Participants Differently	Get Your Participants to Think for Themselves

Most of us have assembled a piece of furniture from a box of parts following a manual full of diagrams with no supporting text. In a similar way, *In the Picture* is about explaining the activity to your group using only diagrams.

Although time consuming to set up, *In the Picture* gives a real sense of independence to participants, as you need to talk to them much less and they can get on with the activity and monitor their own progress. If you work with participants who speak a range of languages, this is a useful strategy.

One real strength of *In the Picture* is that it forces you to think through the task you want the participants to tackle really carefully, and to break it down into steps you can illustrate. You will need to think through all the ways in which your instructions could be misinterpreted, because you can guarantee they will, either accidentally or mischievously.

Once you have the instructions drawn, you can reuse them for many groups, which can pay back the original effort. If your talents in drawing aren't up to the task, it is possible to use annotated photos instead. Resist the urge to produce a lengthy manual unless you have to. Keep it simple and try to only include what you think your participants will need. It's up to you how strict you are about the 'no text' rule, sometimes some numbers or a brief warning are useful additions.

The strategy in action

Ruth is a physics teacher and her class is learning about electric motors. She decides she would like them to build a motor from parts so they understand how they work.

She starts from scratch herself and builds a motor, drawing diagrams for each stage of the process, and assembles them into an instruction manual.

When her class arrives, they are given a tray of parts, with the manual in it, and they are able to get straight on with the task without a lengthy introduction from her.

Ruth passes the manual onto her colleagues in her department to be used with other classes and in future years.

DOI: 10.4324/9781003221296-16

How does this strategy maximise learning?

- *In the Picture* forces you to think through your activity carefully in advance, making sure that most 'diversions' participants might take are cut off.
- By having instructions to follow, participants are encouraged to learn to follow a process.
- This strategy changes your role from the person who is setting the task to one that can work alongside the participants, or to observe them with minimal interaction.
- A well-written set of instructions contains all the information a group needs to complete the activity, reducing their need to ask questions or seek advice, and a requirement on you to answer them!

Pitfalls

- Giving complete instructions for an activity reduces the need for the participants to solve their problems.
- Some activities may be very tricky to draw diagrams for, and it can be a poor way of providing vital safety information.
- Creating illustrated instructions is very time consuming, which may be an issue if they are only used a handful of times.

If you are looking at this you might like to consider...

- Listen Very Carefully
- Mime Artist
- Mysterious Voice
- Written Brief

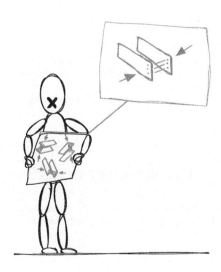

Instruction Manual

Have the group create an instruction manual alongside the activity to help others succeed

Use this strategy to...

Help Your Participants See the Big Picture	Encourage Your Participants to Reflect and Review Well	Help Your Participants Plan and Organise

There is an old adage that you only really understand a topic when you can explain it to someone else. By getting your participants to create an *Instruction Manual* for the activity they are doing, you can help them to consider it from a novice's perspective, which should increase their depth of understanding of it. This is particularly powerful if you have participants who have moved on from being novices themselves and have some basic grasp of the activity.

The *Instruction Manual* doesn't have to be a complicated or complete guide to the activity, and it may concern itself more with behaviour and attitudes than technical expertise. It is easier for participants to recommend practical advice for the task they have taken part in, but it might be more beneficial to recommend useful behaviours, which hopefully your participants can also take on to their own future activities.

The act of producing an *Instruction Manual* requires the participants to notice their actions as they take them and to reflect on them after they have finished. It could take place as part of a formal reflective process, or as a 'fun' finish to an activity. It can be used either at the end of a single activity, or at the end of a series of activities to help participants reflect on and capture the learning they have achieved.

If you want to avoid requiring your participants to write lots of prose, you could ask for top tips from each of them, or get them to draw a diagram explaining their thoughts. Each participant can gather their thoughts individually, or it could be a group exercise; there is merit in both approaches.

The value in creating an *Instruction Manual* comes mostly from the creation of it rather than the using of it by others. That's not to say that 'top tips' from one group to another have no value, but this is mostly a reflective strategy.

The strategy in action

Nick has been teaching sales and negotiation skills for two hours a week to a group of 17-year-old apprentices. At the start of the 12-week programme, which involves theory, discussion, practical exercises and self-reflection. He tells them the final exercise they will do will be to produce a short handbook, which contains advice for future apprentices. Not only will they all receive a copy of this book, but copies will be sent to their managers and the programme director.

At the end of each session, he encourages them to reflect on what they have learnt and to make some notes for the book. In the final session, they organise an editorial process for the notes and produce their book. Nick takes their manuscript and has copies made and bound into a nice booklet.

Each participant receives a copy as a *Souvenir*, and the programme director writes to thank them for the copy they received and to commend them on the wise advice inside.

DOI: 10.4324/9781003221296-17

How does this strategy maximise learning?

- By its very nature, *Instruction Manual* requires significant reflection from participants which will help deepen their learning from an activity and provide an active reminder of it.
- By committing their reflections to an *Instruction Manual*, participants are required to clarify their thoughts, fill any gaps in their knowledge and clear up any lingering misunderstandings from the activity.
- If participants know that their learning is going to be passed on to others, they may feel a sense of responsibility and engagement in the activity.
- If the participant's *Instruction Manual* is of sufficient calibre that it can be used with those who are taking part in the same activity later, it provides a neat piece of peer-to-peer learning which is likely to have a high impact.

Pitfalls

- Creating an *Instruction Manual* may be challenging for those who don't find writing or communication easy.
- Deep reflection of the sort required by this strategy is time consuming and requires some maturity on the part of the participants and risks being a token gesture if not fully committed to.
- If you commit to passing the *Instruction Manual* on to future learners in order to help participants to engage, there is a risk that its contents may be inappropriate, weak or unhelpful.

If you are looking at this you might like to consider...

The Bigger Picture

Islands of Safety

Allow chaos between controlled points

Use this strategy to...

Empower Your Participants	Challenge Your Participants	Have Your Participants Play and Experiment	Build Participants' Confidence

In many activities, you aim to start with a lot of control over your participants and then relinquish increasing amounts of this control as their skill and confidence increases.

If you are starting from a tightly controlled environment, it can be a step too far to give your participants complete *Free Rein*. By building *Islands of Safety* into the activity, you can allow them to act freely between points where you take back control. This gives you 'known' points during a session, which allow you to pause and check that everything is okay before you let your participants loose again.

Islands of Safety can be used to control risk, for example, allowing participants to navigate in easier areas on a walk, taking over for hazardous sections, before returning to the map when the danger is passed. It can also be used to keep an activity on track. Setting times when everyone must return to a certain place allows you to start the next section of the activity on time, assuming everyone turns up! The final use is to help control the learning that happens; you might allow a conversation to develop for a few minutes, before gently interrupting and posing a new question or topic.

The 'islands' don't need to be physical places, they can be fixed at times or upon completion of certain activities. It could be as simple as saying 'I'll pop back in half an hour to check on your progress' or 'Let me know when you have finished part four and we'll see how you are getting on'.

This strategy can benefit both you and your participants. Your participants gain freedom to take control over the activity they are doing, knowing there is a moment in the future when you will be available to pick up the pieces if need be. You benefit from knowing there will be time in the near future where you can take back control if you wish to do so. You do have to accept the risk that between your 'islands' there might be chaos, and have a plan for that.

You can let your participants know you are using *Islands of Safety* with them, or you can quietly use it as a tool without drawing their attention to it. Neither method is better and it is a judgement to be made by you.

The strategy in action

Tim is descending from the summit of a mountain with a group of 10 year olds, headed for their bus in the car park below. They still have a few kilometres to go, but the team have worked well and have proved trustworthy.

Tim knows the route ahead well and it is clearly marked, so he gathers the group and says they may walk at their own pace as long as they stay in a minimum of pairs. The participants are visibly excited at this opportunity to have some freedom.

To maintain some control, Tim asks them to stop when they get to the first trees, about two kilometres ahead, and to wait until the whole group is together again. He walks at the back and upon arrival at the trees,

DOI: 10.4324/9781003221296-18

checks that everybody is present and okay. He also asks them to describe what it feels like to walk at the front of the group, and at the back, to help them think about things from other people's perspectives.

He then sets them off again, this time asking them to stop when they get to the small lake. He has a similar conversation there, before setting them off a final time to the bus.

How does this strategy maximise learning?

♀ *Islands of Safety* can be useful to help a group build confidence in themselves. It can also be useful for building your confidence in them, allowing you to move your 'islands' further apart until eventually you allow them *Free Rein*.

♀ Where there are elements of an activity that have safety concerns, your 'islands' can be positioned before these start.

♀ In a multi-stage activity, this strategy is useful when you need a group to complete one task in order to complete a later part of the activity. You can then position your 'islands' near these parts to help maintain control.

Pitfalls

⚠ You must be willing to accept that there may be chaos between your *Islands of Safety*.

⚠ If your 'islands' are too close together, the participants might feel they are being watched too closely and resent the interruption.

⚠ If you are trying to reduce your participants' dependency on you, having frequent 'islands' can reinforce the feeling that you will always be there to pick up the pieces if it goes wrong.

If you are looking at this you might like to consider...

🔭 Abandon
🔭 Drag and Drop
🔭 Free Rein

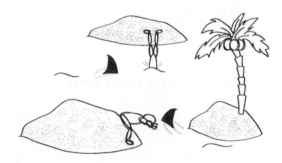

Iterative Goals

Assign the group a series of achievable steps until they reach their goal

Use this strategy to...

Motivate Your Participants	Get Your Participants Setting Goals	Make It Likely Your Participants Will Succeed

Sometimes, when you set a challenging goal for your participants, it can be exciting but seem overwhelming to them. By using *Iterative Goals* you can help them make a series of small steps, until reaching the goal is only another small step away.

The key to using this strategy successfully is to be able to set goals small enough to be attainable, but large enough to make progress. It is best used where progress is clearly measurable and defined milestones can be described and set.

Each *Iterative Goal* can be treated as a success in its own right, with appropriate celebration and reward. This helps to overcome the demotivation that can occur when a big goal feels inaccessible. There is an art to selecting the right number of steps so that each one feels like progress, but the participants are never overwhelmed.

Frequently, you may not know how many small steps you will need to take to reach the main goal when you start. However, if the task is well defined, it may be possible to predict each small goal before you start. This can be helpful if you want participants to understand the big picture and be able to monitor their progress towards the main goal, which can be empowering and help them feel in control.

It is possible for you to set the *Iterative Goals* for the group, or, if they are the right level of competence and maturity, your role can be to help them set their own small steps. Both methods have their own advantages.

The strategy in action

Wanda is running an amateur choir made up of members of the community she lives in. For their Christmas performance, she decides they will perform Handel's *Messiah*, which she knows they will find challenging, but hopes they will enjoy.

When she gathers them together, announces her choice and plays them a professional recording of the piece, there is significant concern from her singers that they will not be good enough to do it justice.

Rather than focus on getting the whole piece correct from the beginning, she starts by handing them a single piece of paper with the chorus on it. They practice this repeatedly, until they are happy with it. At that point she adds the first verse and they practice it, before singing both parts together.

When they feel happy with their performance, she keeps adding sections until they can sing the whole piece. Much to their surprise they are comfortable, proud of what they have achieved and ready for their public show.

DOI: 10.4324/9781003221296-19

How does this strategy maximise learning?

- ♀ When a task feels overwhelming, *Iterative Goals* helps break it down to achievable steps allowing the participants to feel in control.
- ♀ By frequently achieving milestones, groups can celebrate their successes often, leading to a motivated and happy team.
- ♀ Clearly defined steps allow participants to see the bigger picture, allowing them to monitor their progress towards a large goal and make better decisions.

Pitfalls

- ⚠ If you provide the *Iterative Goals*, the participants are never forced to analyse the activity themselves, which can reduce the learning.
- ⚠ By breaking a large goal into smaller challenges, you can reduce the resilience a team might have to develop if they were required to push on through without these steps.
- ⚠ If you misjudge the challenge in one of your smaller goals, and your participants struggle to achieve it, you might make the final goal feel further away, not closer.

If you are looking at this you might like to consider...

- 🔍 How High
- 🔍 Leg Up

Leg Up

Give your participants the minimum amount of support needed to achieve their goal

Use this strategy to...

Build Participants' Confidence	Make It Likely Your Participants Will Succeed

With a challenging activity, groups are unlikely to achieve their full potential without assistance from their instructor or teacher. However, too much help from 'experts' will lessen the experience that participants have, making a successful outcome feel like it was a foregone conclusion and not a result of their efforts.

If you are trying to get a friend over a high wall, you might give them a '*leg up*' so they can reach the top and then pull themselves over. When running activities, this strategy is the equivalent, where you provide just enough help at key moments to place the group's goal within their reach.

By carefully monitoring the progress of the group, you provide small bits of help, hints into the discussion, and provide the minimum assistance required to get the group to the next stage of the challenge. Done subtly, the group should feel they have achieved the goal themselves without feeling like they had to rely on you.

This strategy obviously requires significant judgement, and it is better to err on the side of smaller 'hints' that can be expanded later than giving too much help early on.

The strategy in action

Sam is running a treasure hunt for the ten year olds at the summer school where he works. Each clue directs the group to somewhere else on the campus where the next clue can be found.

The clues are challenging, but the children manage to solve the first few with some effort. However, they get stuck on clue four, which is a coded message. Sam judges that they don't have the knowledge to solve this type of code and so drops small hints into the discussion, guiding them towards the method for decrypting the clue.

They do so, and with a cheer they head off to find the next clue. Progress on this one is smooth. As it appears that his *Leg Up* has been successful, Sam stays quiet, letting the group solve the remaining clues through their own efforts.

DOI: 10.4324/9781003221296-20

How does this strategy maximise learning?

♀ If you use *Leg Up* well, it leaves the participants with the feeling that they have achieved their goal through their own efforts.

♀ It allows you to keep an exercise or task 'flowing', which is useful for your group's motivation and your time-keeping.

♀ You remain outside the activity monitoring the group's progress, giving you space to observe and understand the dynamics and characteristics of the participants.

Pitfalls

⚠ You need to exercise careful judgement to know exactly when the group requires a *Leg Up* and when they should be left to keep trying.

⚠ Once you have decided to intervene, *Leg Up* requires significant judgement about what is the minimum amount of help the group requires, too much and it becomes full scale assistance rather than just a leg up!

⚠ If a group knows you are there to provide a 'leg up' when they are struggling, it can reduce the sense of independence that the team feel.

If you are looking at this you might like to consider...

🔭 Cheerleader
🔭 Help for Sale
🔭 Life Lines
🔭 Wind Up and Let Go

Lifelines

Give the group a limit on the number of times they can ask for help

Use this strategy to...

Encourage Your Participants to Solve Problems	Encourage Your Participants to Use Questions Well

Sometimes your participants get into the habit of asking for help, which may be the easiest solution, but often results in a reduction in their learning. One way to encourage them to consider how often they ask for help is to limit the number of times they can do so.

Where an activity is safe enough to allow, you can offer your participants a fixed number of *Lifelines*. Each lifeline can be traded for the answer to one question. When they are out of lifelines, they must continue with no further help from you.

There are a number of creative ways in which you can use this strategy. Participants may be given physical tokens, which must be handed over each time to gain the information required. Participants may need to submit their question in writing, so that they are forced to think carefully before committing to using one of their lifelines. Alternatively, you may wish to limit them to 'closed' questions that can only be answered with a yes or no.

It can be powerful to limit who can use a *Lifeline* to have a question answered. You can allow a free-for-all where anyone can use one, or if you have a leader, you can limit it to them. Alternatively, you can require a successful vote of all participants. Each has its benefits and drawbacks depending on what you are trying to achieve.

It's possible to use this strategy to make an activity easier or harder for different ability groups by setting the number of lifelines before you start. It is also possible to give additional support during an exercise by allowing the group to find or earn another *Lifeline*.

The strategy in action

Lucy is working with her youth organisation, running an evening session for 11–14 year olds, helping them understand how they interact in a team.

She gives them 20 sheets of paper, one roll of tape and some scissors and asks them to design and build a bridge that spans a half metre gap between two tables. Their goal is to make the bridge support as much weight as possible.

Once she has explained what they have to do and put some notes on the white board, she gives each team three bottle tops with question marks drawn on them, and explains that if they want to ask a question, they must trade a bottle top for the answer. If they run out of bottle tops, they have run out of questions.

Some groups use their bottle tops straight away, and some still have some left at the end of the session. At times there seemed to be more discussion about the bottle tops than there was about the bridge designs, which gives Lucy and the team plenty to talk about when they examine their team dynamics.

DOI: 10.4324/9781003221296-21

How does this strategy maximise learning?

- Knowing you only have a certain amount of *Lifelines* will encourage groups to think for themselves before they ask for help.
- This strategy makes the group think hard about when to ask their questions and what to ask. This helps them learn to form good questions, and in the process they will probably solve some of them themselves.
- *Lifelines* is a good way to support multiple groups, as you can position yourself as a 'central help desk'.
- With a limited number of *Lifelines*, the participants will have to balance the 'cost' of getting help against the potential benefit, much like in real life.

Pitfalls

- Your participants may feel deserted if they use up their *Lifelines* and are still stuck.
- If you misjudge how much help, and therefore how many *Lifelines*, your group will need, you must accept that the activity may not get completed.
- As with all strategies where you hand over some control to the participants, you run the risk of the activity not being completed.

If you are looking at this you might like to consider...

- Help for Sale
- Leg Up
- Questioner

Listen Very Carefully

Give instructions for the task only once

Use this strategy to...

Brief Your Participants Differently	Get Your Participants to Think for Themselves	Ensure Your Participants Support Each Other

One way to ensure that your participants pay close attention to the information you are giving them is to offer it once only, for example, reading a set of instructions out loud one time at the start of the activity. You must make it clear to them that this is their only chance to hear this information, because if it comes as a surprise to them later, it can be frustrating and make them cross with you.

Giving a group one chance to get the information, should engage them right from the start and encourage them to pay attention to the details. It also allows for an element of teamwork as they piece together the bits that each one remembers. Groups can also feel trusted and empowered as they are given the task once and allowed to get on with it.

Your brief must be accurate and contain all the information the group needs to undertake the activity, because once it is underway, you shouldn't answer any questions or give any information a second time. It can be useful to write the information down as that forces you to consider through every part of the activity to ensure that you have thought of everything they may need to know. You can then read it out to ensure you don't miss anything.

It may be that with a complicated set of instructions, you may give them twice or even three times, but you must make it clear from the beginning which of these it will be. For some groups it may be helpful to give them the means of capturing the information, either on paper or by recording it, although this can diminish the 'high stakes' of giving it only once.

This strategy must be used extremely carefully with activities with any degree of risk. One method to mitigate this is to simply step in with 'I'm going to stop you there, you aren't following the instructions' and then only letting them continue once they rectify the issue.

The strategy in action

Maggie is teaching cookery as part of a life skills program for young people who have moved out of home for the first time. She takes them to a supermarket to shop for ingredients, and before they go in she stops and tells them to *Listen Very Carefully*, because she is only going to explain the next step once.

She says to them they have a budget of £15 between them. They need to shop for three courses, all of which must require cooking. Nothing may come from a tin, the main course must have at least two vegetables in it and at least one item of protein, and the pudding must be something that everybody will like. The starter and pudding must be able to be prepared in advance. They have thirty minutes to get everything they will need.

She then sets them off into the shop and waits by the till with £15 in cash, looking forward to finding out what they will be eating that evening!

DOI: 10.4324/9781003221296-22

How does this strategy maximise learning?

💡 Having to *Listen Very Carefully* and remember the instructions given means the 'active' part of an activity starts at the very beginning, engaging participants straightaway.

💡 This strategy can deliver a real feeling of jeopardy—failure to listen means failure at the task, without any physical risk.

💡 Participants must work together to recall the information, which can both strengthen teamwork and lead to disagreements that require resolution.

💡 Groups feel trusted and empowered as they are given the task once and allowed to get on with it.

Pitfalls

⚠️ If a group fails to *Listen Very Carefully* they will inevitably fail to achieve their goal. There is no opportunity to rectify any early errors, and they can often complete a different task to the one expected.

⚠️ In high risk activities, if you do not repeat your instructions, you lose the chance to repeat safety information when it is most pertinent.

⚠️ If you introduce this strategy carelessly or insensitively, and the participants fail to understand its purpose, you risk appearing awkward and unhelpful, which can damage your relationship with the group.

⚠️ This strategy is particularly difficult for participants who have short-term memory difficulties.

If you are looking at this you might like to consider...

🔍 In the Picture
🔍 Mime Artist
🔍 Mysterious Voice
🔍 Written Brief

Mime Artist

Demonstrate the whole task without words or sounds, exaggerating key points

Use this strategy to...

Brief Your Participants Differently	Challenge Your Participants	Get Your Participants to Think for Themselves

When introducing activities, especially ones that are very physical, it is normal to include a demonstration. While talking can provide clarity to your demonstrations, it can also distract participants from watching carefully. By becoming a *Mime Artist*, and not speaking at all, you can focus their attention on what you are doing and reduce the number of senses through which they are receiving information.

You can introduce the demonstration by speaking, or even in mime itself, using actions like pointing to your eyes and then to the group to signal that they need to watch. It is important to ensure that you have your group's full attention before you start, and once you do so, they will often be intrigued enough to stay engaged. The change from listening to watching is a useful tool to retain participant's interest, especially if you are having to do a number of demonstrations in quick succession.

Your demonstration should not only be clear, but should exaggerate key parts of the activity, and theatrical facial expressions can help add emotion and emphasise important messages. Resist the urge to get too ambitious, keep your mime limited to 'how to do this'; the simpler it can be the better.

Mime Artist works best for short activities that are predominantly physical with limited decisions to make and that can be demonstrated in their entirety within a couple of minutes. It may be worth repeating your mime a second time so that, once participants understand what the end result is supposed to be, they can focus on the details that will get them there.

The strategy in action

Susie is a leader with a youth organisation who are teaching outdoor skills to children ages 10–14. This session they are learning to light fires without matches.

Susie gathers her group around her and uses the universal signal for 'watch this' by pointing to the group, then to her eyes, then to a little tin on the floor at her feet. The group falls silent and are intrigued by what it contains.

She silently opens the tin, and without speaking, extracts some cotton wool and a flint and steel. She holds up the cotton wool and looks across the group before pulling at it to fluff it up. She strokes the bundle on her cheek to show how soft it has become, and smiles broadly to show this is good.

She places the cotton wool in her fireplace and picks up the flint and steel, showing it to the group. She demonstrates it, first by miming overly exaggerated, slow actions, then she uses it properly to make sparks in the air. Finally she holds the flint and steel over the cotton wool, and sets light to it with the sparks.

Without speaking she has demonstrated the first part of lighting a fire, and she dismisses her group with a pushing away gesture. The participants head off to give it a go.

DOI: 10.4324/9781003221296-23

How does this strategy maximise learning?

- Becoming a *Mime Artist* adds an element of fun and really encourages groups to pay attention right from the start!
- The change from spoken introductions to one in mime can help retain participant's interest.
- This strategy can 'bring to life' an activity and help engage visual learners.
- Watching a *Mime Artist*, dissuades participants from asking lots of questions as they know you won't answer them!

Pitfalls

- You must have the participants' attention before you use this strategy, otherwise they won't notice your demonstration.
- This strategy is hard to use with activities that are complicated, require decisions or lack physical elements. You must be able to demonstrate the task clearly.
- Although this strategy can be effective, you must be confident that your participants want to engage with your 'pantomime'. If they are disengaged, they might just find it silly, and the whole thing can feel like a joke to them.

If you are looking at this you might like to consider...

- In the Picture
- Listen Very Carefully
- Mysterious Voice
- Written Brief

Mysterious Voice

Play audio instructions with all the information needed and leave the group to follow them

Use this strategy to...

Empower Your Participants	Brief Your Participants Differently

A change in the way instructions are delivered can help participants engage. In this strategy, the instructions for the activity are given to the group in an entirely audio format, not by you, but by a *Mysterious Voice*. This might be a recording, a telephone call, a radio message or even an 'overheard' conversation.

The participants may be aware of the identity of the person that is talking, or it might be a truly *Mysterious Voice*. If it is recorded, participants can listen to the message as many times as they like, a phone or radio call is a one-off event, so they must *Listen Very Carefully*.

There is a skill in extracting information from audio, which is valuable in its own right. The fact that the participants can't ask questions means they can only work with the information they are given, forcing them to solve any problems without outside assistance.

One real strength of *Mysterious Voice* is that it forces you to think through the task you want the participants to tackle really carefully, and to break it down into steps you can present through audio. Try to think through all the ways in which your recording could be misinterpreted, because you can guarantee it will be, either accidentally or maliciously.

Mysterious Voice can be a really creative way of adding a 'story' over the top of the activity, perhaps as part of a *Bigger Picture*.

The strategy in action

Adrian is a teacher at a school. He has been given a week to teach them about working alongside each other in challenging situations. He decides the week will have an 'astronaut training' theme.

When the students arrive on day three of the programme, he plays them a recorded 'radio message' from the International Space Station. Through the static, it says that to test a new camera onboard as part of NASA's science programme, they need five beacons of different colours to be placed at five locations around the school. The message contains the coordinates, colour and time at which the beacons must be in place.

The students scramble to write down the information, before making a plan and heading out to place beacons in their correct places.

DOI: 10.4324/9781003221296-24

How does this strategy maximise learning?

- *Mysterious Voice* forces you to think through your activity carefully in advance, making sure that most 'diversions' participants might take are cut off.
- This strategy changes your role from the person who is setting the task, to one that can work alongside the participants, or to observe them with minimal interaction.
- A well-presented set of instructions contains all the information a group needs to complete the activity, reducing their need to ask questions or seek advice.
- Hearing instructions from a *Mysterious Voice* can be fun and engaging for participants.
- Finding or discovering an audio message can lead a group onto the next part of an activity without any intervention from you.

Pitfalls

- Giving complete instructions for an activity at the start reduces the need for the participants to solve their problems.
- Some activities may be very tricky to describe out loud or might require demonstrations, and audio can be a poor way of providing vital safety information.
- Creating instructions that cannot be easily misunderstood is tricky, and the participants may end up interpreting them in a completely different way than you expected.
- If you have to step in to clarify or explain something to participants, you break the illusion of separation between you and the *Mysterious Voice*.

If you are looking at this you might like to consider...

- In the Picture
- Listen Very Carefully
- Storyteller
- The Bigger Picture

Peer Expert

Teach one or more of the group the skills they need and get them to teach the others

Use this strategy to...

Make Your Participants Think about Each Other and Their Differences	Build Participants' Confidence	Ensure Your Participants Support Each Other

It can be a very empowering experience to stand in front of a group of peers and teach them. Where an activity contains a discrete skill that can be learnt relatively quickly, you can teach that skill to one of the participants and send them back to the group to pass it on as a *Peer Expert*.

When participants know they will be teaching their peers, there is a real incentive to learn a skill well so they can appear competent. This vulnerability encourages them to ensure that they pay attention and practice until they are happy. Participants often enjoy the role of a *Peer Expert* and the responsibility this gives them.

Participants often respond better to being taught by an 'equal' than by a 'pro'. It is likely that the language a *Peer Expert* uses and the demonstrations they give will be much closer to a novice's version of the skill and can feel much more accessible.

You might have more than one *Peer Expert* for an activity. If you are working with lots of people who need a single skill, it is useful to train several participants to pass on that skill. If your activity requires several skills to complete, you may also choose to have several *Peer Experts*, but this time they are each competent in one of the skills needed.

You must use this strategy carefully and monitor your *Peer Experts* to ensure that they are passing on the skills to a standard that allows the activity to continue and to continue safely.

The strategy in action

Jessica is a senior doctor who has responsibility for teaching the next generation of medical students.

One day she asks two students to come to her office, where she explains that she is going to teach them to take a medical history, and that the next day they will be teaching this skill to their peers. She takes them through the process, teaches them a mnemonic to help them remember it and allows them to practice on her. Finally she shares some tips for teaching the skill.

The next day she meets all her students before the ward rounds. Her two *Peer Experts* take over the morning session and begin to teach their newly acquired skill. Jessica monitors them from the back, coffee in hand, occasionally injecting with helpful information, taking care not to undermine the teaching.

The medical students enjoy being taught by their peers for once, and feel more comfortable asking questions of an equal than they do of their superiors.

DOI: 10.4324/9781003221296-25

How does this strategy maximise learning?

- Teaching others as a *Peer Expert* helps to reinforce a participant's learning and personal understanding.
- Groups react well to being taught by a peer because the language used and the demonstrations given are likely to be much closer to a novice's version of the skill.
- This strategy allows the group a sense of completing the task as a team, and questions are directed to the *Peer Expert* not to you, encouraging problem solving and allowing you to be an observer.
- Having *Peer Experts* creates a role for members of the group to take on some leadership and also allows you to create 'champions' in your group who will help you motivate the rest.

Pitfalls

- If your *Peer Expert* forgets or alters some of the information you have taught them, or doesn't give good explanations, they may well teach a version of the skill that is less effective or unhelpful.
- Groups can have too much confidence in their *Peer Expert*, even though they might have just learnt the skill and may lack confidence themselves. You run the risk of them being 'blamed' if the activity isn't successful.
- Teaching and coaching is an art that you have developed over many years. *Peer Experts* will likely lack those skills and their teaching may be ineffective and not very inspiring.

If you are looking at this you might like to consider...

- Delegate
- Hidden Agendas
- Secret Agent

Playtime

Allow the group to learn through play by setting only necessary boundaries

Use this strategy to...

Encourage Your Participants to Solve Problems	Have Your Participants Play and Experiment	Get Your Participants Setting Goals

We often think of play as an activity for younger children, but it is a powerful tool for any age group. Where your activity has broad goals, such as getting to know an area or innovating solutions, allowing your participants to have some *Playtime*, can give them the chance to make discoveries for themselves.

When participants learn by making discoveries for themselves, their understanding is often greater and the learning is more likely to stick than when it comes from someone else.

Playtime is not simply abandoning your participants to their own learning, it is a conscious strategy which requires thought to use. Choosing the right environment, tools, language and time all play a part in allowing your participants to make the discoveries you hope they do. Similarly, while you want the 'play' to be as unrestricted as possible, you will likely have to set some boundaries to address safety, logistics and other practicalities.

Given the freedom to play, participants can choose the direction their own learning takes. You can be open with them about what you hope they will learn, or simply allow them to play with no explanation. Younger participants are often more happy just to go for it, older ones may want to understand why they are being given this freedom.

If you do want to provide some advice while *Playtime* is happening, you can interact one-to-one as a participant needs it. This allows your coaching to be timely and tailored to individuals, while the other participants get on with 'playing'.

If you finish your *Playtime* by asking participants to share something they have learnt with the group, they can all benefit from each other's learning as well as their own discoveries.

The strategy in action

Bertie is coaching adults who have joined his hockey club but who have never played the game before. He welcomes them onto the pitch and gives them each a hockey stick and a ball.

Rather than explaining what to do with them, he asks them to go and experiment. The only limits he sets for them are that they must stay on the pitch if possible, that they should only use the flat face of the stick, and that the head of the stick mustn't be lifted above waist height. He points out where the goals are and that he has scattered some training cones around.

Slightly nervously the novices head out onto the pitch and have a go at controlling the ball with varying levels of success. Some head for the goal, some try to go in a straight line and two decide to have a go at passing to each other.

While they do so, Bertie wanders around making small suggestions to individuals to help them improve. After twenty minutes he calls them all back over to him, and asks each one to share with the group something they have discovered.

DOI: 10.4324/9781003221296-26

How does this strategy maximise learning?

- By making discoveries for themselves, participants' understanding is often greater and the learning is more likely to stick than when it comes from someone else.
- In the right environment, *Playtime* is very engaging, as long as participants understand why it is happening.
- This strategy allows participants to control their own learning, choosing what to take interest in and whether, and with whom, to collaborate.
- While *Playtime* is happening, it provides a good opportunity to provide one-to-one tailored coaching or conversation, without disrupting the rest of a group.

Pitfalls

- ⚠ *Playtime* requires careful set up and use if you require specific learning to happen. It is entirely possible to get some very random outcomes!
- ⚠ *Playtime* only works well for activities where knowledge and skills are realistically discoverable by your participants on their own. If it is too complicated, they may never progress without your help.
- ⚠ In hazardous areas, or for activities that require lots of safety information, it may be inappropriate to allow *Playtime*.

If you are looking at this you might like to consider...

- Abandon
- Free Rein
- Islands of Safety
- Wind Up and Let Go

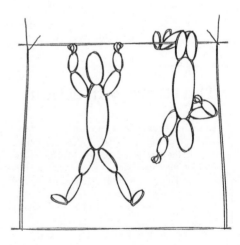

Plot Spoiler

Tell the group what they can expect to learn before they do the task

Use this strategy to...

Encourage Your Participants to Reflect and Review Well	Help Your Participants See the Big Picture

Activities often produce a range of learning outcomes for a group or individuals within that group. Sometimes you want to make the learning more predictable, and that is when a *Plot Spoiler* can help.

A *Plot Spoiler* is when you clearly explain the learning that you hope your participants will get from the activity before you start. When you have done so, they will be primed to look for that learning as they undertake the activity, and will naturally make it a focus of any review.

This approach is valuable when you expect the activity to be slightly chaotic, there are lots of possible learning outcomes or you expect the interactions between participants to be complicated. This narrowing of your focus to a unifying thread guides thoughts, conversations and actions during the activity. This helps keep learning 'on-track' and headed towards your desired learning outcomes.

Giving a *Plot Spoiler* is also useful when you want the participants to focus on learning that isn't the same as the goal of the activity. By making clear what the learning goal is in advance, you help avoid the participants getting so wrapped up in the activity that they forget to think about what they are learning.

A second running of the same activity with the same participants can be given a totally different focus by providing a different *Plot Spoiler*, making it a different learning experience.

The strategy in action

Lorna runs a gospel choir who have a concert coming up. She has chosen a piece of music that she knows they will find challenging, but it is a joyful piece and she is confident that they can perform it well.

As the concert approaches, they have been working hard on a certain technical part of the song which many in the choir have to concentrate hard for. She notices that while they are hitting the right notes, this section of the song is feeling flat and lacks emotion.

At the next rehearsal, she starts by explaining the problem and asking the choir to focus on smiling and feeling the emotion in this bit of the song. She makes it clear that she doesn't mind if they don't quite hit the notes, they can work on that next time.

By giving the choir only one thing to focus on, being joyful, they relax and produce a piece of music that sounds much more in keeping with their goal and the style of the song. Technically, they still have some work to do, but by providing a *Plot Spoiler* she has removed an issue that was hampering their performance.

DOI: 10.4324/9781003221296-27

How does this strategy maximise learning?

- Providing a *Plot Spoiler* allows focus on a single piece of learning, maximising the chances of it happening.
- Complicated situations can be broken down into single learning goals for each activity, helping focus participants' thoughts and actions.

Pitfalls

- By providing a *Plot Spoiler*, you are altering the way in which a task happens, and participants may alter their natural behaviour to meet the given objectives.
- By focusing on only one outcome, you risk trivialising complicated experiences and disengaging participants.
- If you provide a *Plot Spoiler* before you start, you don't always get to address the learning that actually happens, just what you set up in advance. You may be forced to choose which of these to discuss.

If you are looking at this you might like to consider...

- Fishbowl
- Hidden Agendas

Pulling Strings

Adapt the activity without the group's knowledge to make it easier or harder

Use this strategy to...

| Motivate Your Participants | Challenge Your Participants | Build Participants' Confidence |

Finding the right level of challenge for a group of participants can be tricky, especially if you don't know them well. It is a useful skill to be able to *Pull Strings* in the background to adjust your activity so that it provides the right level of challenge, without the changes being obvious to those taking part.

You may wish to make your activity easier to ensure the participants' success without reducing their sense of achievement or damaging their morale. Alternatively, you may make it harder to provide a greater challenge and ensure that they feel they have achieved.

Used well, your group should never know that you were *Pulling Strings* in the background. It can be hard to do this seamlessly, but knowing your activity well and introducing it carefully, allowing for flexibility later, will help. It is easier to use this strategy without alerting your group if you think about places where you can adjust your activity before you start, but it is also possible to make these changes along the way, if it becomes appropriate.

This strategy is particularly useful when you don't know how able your group is when you start the activity. You can spend some time getting to understand how capable they are before committing to a certain level of challenge. This is commonly the case when you are either on the first session with your participants or when you only have them for one session.

The strategy in action

Rupert is a mountain guide who has been asked by a family of four to help them have an adventure in the mountains.

He proposes that they follow a ridge that links several mountains and is a well-known route in the area. He hasn't climbed with this family before but he knows that there are several descent routes from different points along the ridge, allowing him to alter the level of challenge as he goes along. He deliberately avoids giving a list of the mountains they will climb, but instead focuses on the challenge, adventure and fun they will have on the journey.

The day starts with a long ascent then the party makes their way along the ridge. The family are capable and move well so Rupert is able to continue past the first two descent routes and continue. After lunch, one of the children begins to tire, so he opts to take the next route back to the valley, missing out the last peak.

Once back at their vehicles, the family are overjoyed at having 'completed' the ridge, unaware that there was one more mountain they could have done but having had the adventure they wanted.

DOI: 10.4324/9781003221296-28

How does this strategy maximise learning?

- ♀ Used well, *Pulling Strings* can virtually ensure your participants complete the activity they are doing.
- ♀ By discreetly making activities easier you can help increase your participants' morale without them feeling like their original goal has been cheapened.
- ♀ You can ensure a competent group is appropriately challenged and gets a sense of achievement by *Pulling Strings* to make an activity harder if they are finding it too easy.
- ♀ This strategy is useful to help keep activities on time or where one activity needs finishing before the next can start.

Pitfalls

- ⚠ It is hard to adjust activities discreetly without knowing the activity well and without setting vague enough goals that allow you to act later, which can make you seem unsure of yourself.
- ⚠ If you are working with more than one group, they might compare their experiences and notice that you have been *Pulling Strings*.
- ⚠ If you get 'caught' *Pulling Strings*, you can lose the trust of your participants. If you are caught making it easier, they might feel that you are reducing their achievement. If you are caught making the activity harder, they may well feel that you are 'against' them.

If you are looking at this you might like to consider...

- 👀 Help for Sale
- 👀 How High
- 👀 Shifting Sands

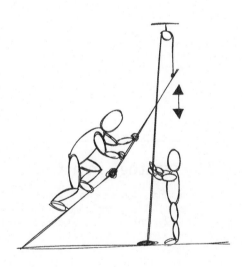

Questioner

Interact with the group by only using questions

Use this strategy to...

Encourage Your Participants to Solve Problems	Challenge Your Participants	Encourage Your Participants to Use Questions Well

One of the key skills of a top performance coach is to be able to ask the right questions of their participants. This strategy takes that idea to its ultimate conclusion, as a *Questioner*, every interaction you have with the group should be in the form of a question.

In order for this to be a useful strategy, you need to think carefully about the questions you ask. There are occasions when very 'open' questions such as 'What do you think?' will be valuable. On other occasions, 'closed' or leading questions such as 'Is this the best route forward?' allow you to add information or 'instructions' into the conversation.

The power in this strategy is that while you are steering their thinking, the participants must do the actual thinking themselves. There is an art to creating a route for them to follow through their own, often chaotic and muddled, thoughts. The level of direction needed in your questions will depend on the ability and maturity of your group. In general it is better to try to use open, broad questions, but on rare occasions you might have to ask very directive questions, such as 'Have you considered doing...?' if you want your group to progress.

Early on in an activity you should be using questions to help them generate and explore options, make sense of a situation, and challenge their own assumptions. Later on you may be steering them towards choosing between options and isolating the information they need to act.

It is important that your participants understand that you are not just asking questions to be annoying! You must be leading their thoughts towards a desired conclusion, and they must feel that is the case and that you are helping them. With very capable participants, you might be able to select one of the group to be the *Questioner* which combines the power of the strategy with an opportunity to stretch individuals.

The strategy in action

Mike is running an introduction to engineering session for his physics students in their final year at school. He gives them an aubergine, two carrots, a red pepper, a parsnip and a potato, along with some cocktail sticks, and challenges them to design and build vegetable cars that must roll down a ramp and travel as far as possible.

He explains that engineering is all about answering questions, so he will only support them during the session by asking questions. Even when his students ask him a question themselves, he replies with one in return.

Early on in the session he asks questions like 'What are your initial ideas?', 'Why do you think that will work?', 'Have you seen anything like this before?' and 'What other areas could you explore?'.

As the students start finalising their designs, he asks, 'How are you going to make this?', 'Have you thought about what tools you might need?' and 'What problems might you face with this design?'.

After the students have raced their vegetable cars, he finishes the session with 'Did you enjoy that?', 'What did you learn during that?' and 'What piece of advice would you give to future vegetable car designers?'.

DOI: 10.4324/9781003221296-29

How does this strategy maximise learning?

- By only asking questions, you make the group think for themselves and empower them to solve problems while still being able to provide guidance.
- Using carefully timed and phrased questions, you can 'steer' an activity without your participants feeling that you are interfering.
- By avoiding direct instructions, you free the group from your preconceived path for the activity and allow them to come up with ideas that you yourself may not have considered.
- Exposing your participants to good questioning might inspire them to think about the power of questions and to begin to form and use them for themselves.

Pitfalls

- It is very easy as a *Questioner* to frustrate and irritate your group, as every question they have is answered with another question!
- It can be tempting to use leading questions to try to get the group to come up with your answer, which can feel very frustrating to participants as they try to 'guess what is in your head'.
- Asking great questions is a real art and requires thought and practice to use well.

If you are looking at this you might like to consider...

- Devil's Advocate
- Devil on the Shoulder
- Lifelines

Saviour

Swoop in at the last minute with the solution or answer to ensure success

Use this strategy to...

Inspire Your Participants	Make It Likely Your Participants Will Succeed

It is very motivating for a group to succeed. There are occasions where you want your participants to have as much control and as little support as possible, but you do need them to complete the activity they are doing.

As a *Saviour*, you can let them get on with it for as long as possible, then if needed, swoop in at the last minute to ensure they are successful. This might take the form of hints towards a solution, corrections to errors made, being an extra pair of hands or supplying useful knowledge.

There is a trade-off to be made between reducing the participants' engagement by taking some of the ownership of the activity away, and motivating them and allowing progress by ensuring their success. That is a judgement you have to make with this strategy.

In an ideal world, you will never have to be a *Saviour*, but it is a useful back-up strategy to have available.

The strategy in action

Toby has organised a camping trip for 12 year olds. He has set it up so they are responsible for as much of the running of the camp as possible, including doing the cooking.

Three participants are responsible for preparing the dinner this evening, and while they are making progress, he can clearly see that they won't be ready by the time the rest of the campers sit down at seven.

Toby monitors their progress until about quarter to seven, when he decides that he is sure they will not be ready on time, and then wanders into the kitchen tent to help. He turns up one of the stoves, shows a participant how to chop up salad, sets one student buttering bread and takes over the draining of the rice. All the time he reassures the students how well they have done and tries to make it seem that he has just popped in to be useful.

With the help of his last minute intervention, the campers are fed on time, and the three students are given a round of applause as they serve their meal proudly.

DOI: 10.4324/9781003221296-30

How does this strategy maximise learning?

- By ensuring success, your participants will be motivated.
- If an activity needs to be completed to allow progress, being a *Saviour* can ensure this happens while still giving the participants freedom.
- This strategy can be used to help your participants build their trust in you, reinforcing that you know what you are talking about and you won't let them down.

Pitfalls

- Sometimes participants will benefit from not succeeding, and this strategy removes their opportunity to learn from any failures.
- Having you swoop in and 'save' them can mean a group feels robbed of the chance to succeed by their own efforts or silly that they were unable to. It also can highlight the difference in ability between you and them. Both of these can leave them demoralised.
- Once you have been a *Saviour* for a group, they may come to expect success, and they can feel let down if you don't do it every time in the future, damaging their trust in you.

If you are looking at this you might like to consider...

- Leg Up
- Pulling Strings
- Shifting Sands
- Wizard

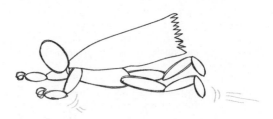

Secret Agent

Assign a secret mission to one team member alongside the group's main task

Use this strategy to...

Empower Your Participants	Make Your Participants Think about Each Other and Their Differences

While running your activity, you can provide more opportunities for learning by assigning one of the participants to be your *Secret Agent*. You give them an alternative or additional goal to the rest of the team for them to try to achieve during the activity.

Depending on what you want them to achieve, there are a variety of secret missions you can set. They can vary from ensuring that everyone is heard in discussions, being the most enthusiastic *Cheerleader* for the group, being a *Devil's Advocate* by questioning everything, or even, with care, being a saboteur trying to stop the rest of the group succeeding.

Having a *Secret Agent* is a great way to introduce ideas or actions into a group without it appearing to come from you. It can also be used to introduce attributes or behaviours that a team is missing to allow it to function better, or to realise the importance of those behaviours. It can be used to challenge and stretch individuals and to introduce harmony, or disharmony into a team to see how it copes.

The *Secret Agent* needs to remain secret. This differentiates this strategy from simply assigning roles to people. The secrecy is important because if the group knows that the agent is acting on your behalf, their behaviour will be different than if they don't.

You must brief your agent on their 'mission' before the task without the other team members knowing. You can assign them a goal, or you can work with them to choose one, or you could even have 'mission cards' with different goals on them and let the agent pick randomly.

You must show caution in using this strategy, as the way the agent operates has a significant effect on the outcome. You must ensure that the agent has sufficient support from you to undertake their missions effectively, and the group trusts you enough to understand your reasons for using this strategy.

The strategy in action

Charlie is in charge of a group of twelve students and four members of staff sharing a hut at a summer camp. In addition to their activities, each day the group must cook their meals, including a sit-down dinner.

They have been together for about a week, and every evening the group have made a series of mistakes, such as starting to prepare the meal too late, not reading the recipes provided, arguing over boring jobs and forgetting to allow for dietary requirements. All of these have been caused by overconfidence and rushing.

DOI: 10.4324/9781003221296-31

Charlie decides that the group will benefit from questioning their own actions more, so he approaches one of the campers, Kala, to be his *Secret Agent*. He asks her to be a *Devil's Advocate*, to challenge what the team is doing. He knows Kala is not only mature, but has the respect of many of the rest of the group and when she talks, they listen. That evening, Kala carefully challenges the group when she sees overconfidence, assumptions being made or arguments starting. As she is part of the group, the team reacts better to these challenges than if Charlie had had to step in.

The meal is prepared more calmly, on time and with less stress as a result of Kala's careful questions. Talking over after dinner cocoa, Charlie asks the team what had changed that resulted in a better meal, and gradually guides their thoughts towards the value of good questions.

How does this strategy maximise learning?

- This allows you to influence a group's behaviour through your *Secret Agent* without seeming to interfere.
- By choosing the right *Secret Agent*, you can provide a challenge to an individual who would benefit from it.
- This strategy can also be used to introduce behaviours that a team is missing to allow it to function better, or for them to realise the importance of those behaviours.

Pitfalls

- With younger or less mature groups, your agent can face negative consequences if they appear to be unhelpful or if they are 'found out'.
- There is the possibility of you losing the trust of your group if you use this strategy more than once and they may be suspicious in future exercises.
- The *Secret Agent* needs to do a competent job of their mission, and be discreet about it or the group will be suspicious and challenge or ignore them.

If you are looking at this you might like to consider...

- Delegate
- Hidden Agenda
- Peer Expert

Shifting Sands

Adapt the activity with the group's knowledge to make it easier or harder

Use this strategy to...

Challenge Your Participants	Motivate Your Participants	Make It Likely Your Participants Will Succeed

If you have only just met a group, or are asking a group to take on a complex activity, it is often difficult to know how well they will do before they start. Some activities allow you to vary the difficulty as you go along which can help manage this situation. For example, a climbing instructor can choose different routes or a fitness coach can alter the weights his clients are using.

By altering the task or the constraints of the task, you can ensure that the group faces the appropriate level of challenge throughout the activity. These changes, making things easier or harder, are not about secret background adjustments, but are done with the group's knowledge and are introduced and carried out with their consent. *Shifting Sands* is about altering the task, not the team completing it.

This is particularly useful for activities that may be run several times, where the phrase 'This time we are going to make it harder by…' can be used to increase the challenge each time. Alternatively, 'That didn't go as we planned, how about we…' can be used to remove a layer of difficulty to ensure successful completion.

Another useful facet of *Shifting Sands* is that, with care, the 'sand' can be shifted by different amounts for different team members. This allows for some differentiation within the group and for each member to be challenged an appropriate amount.

The strategy in action

Kevin is working with a group of adults to produce an amateur dramatic version of *A Midsummer's Night Dream*. He knows they have been learning their lines for a few weeks, and that some are close to knowing them all while others are a little behind. He starts at the beginning of the script and asks everyone to begin by delivering their lines from the first two pages from memory.

As the group moves through the script, they all confidently cope with those pages so he asks them to keep going. By the time they are on the fifth page, two members of the cast are clearly struggling to remember their lines, so he quietly passes them their scripts while the others keep going. Gradually he hands everyone their script so they can complete the first act.

DOI: 10.4324/9781003221296-32

How does this strategy maximise learning?

- *Shifting Sands* is useful when you don't know a group's ability, or the time available is fixed and you want the group to complete an activity.
- In a multi-stage task, a future stage may be reliant on the correct answer from a previous stage and so the group must complete the first stage to progress.
- Sometimes completing an activity by any means possible is more important to the group's dynamic than doing so without outside interference.

Pitfalls

- If you make an activity easier, any feelings of success the group have at the end can be tainted with feelings of 'we only achieved this because you made the task easier, we failed the "real" task'.
- If you make an activity harder in the middle, the group can feel that you are 'against' them.
- If you make an activity harder too many times, the group can get fed-up and lose engagement as they feel it is impossible to 'win'.

If you are looking at this you might like to consider...

- How High
- Leg Up
- Pulling Strings
- Saviour

Souvenir

Distribute a physical memento to each member to remind them of their experience and learning once they are home

Use this strategy to...

Encourage Your Participants to Reflect and Review Well

The transfer of learning from an experience on a programme, course or lesson back to the participants' day-to-day life is one of the trickier parts of creating and running meaningful activities. One solution to this is to ensure they leave with a tangible souvenir of the experience that will remind them of it and bring the learning from it back to mind when they see it in the future.

The souvenir should be a physical object, preferably something aesthetic or useful so that it is kept for a long time. Ideally, the participant will stumble across it in the months and years after the activity, and recall not only a positive experience, but the changes they made because of it. Keyrings, t-shirts, bookmarks, paperweights and mugs are all comparatively cheap to have made and customised with activity details or participants' names.

If the souvenir can be created or customised by the participants themselves, they may hold it in greater affection. It doesn't need to be expensive or grand, in fact, found or made objects can be just as effective. Stones from a beach can be turned into paperweights, parts of a map can be turned into bookmarks, or name badges turned into keyrings. Creating a souvenir of a longer programme can be an activity in its own right.

The presentation of souvenirs can become a focus for the end of an activity or programme, and can provide an excuse to celebrate achievements and reflect on progress made.

The strategy in action

Nia is the director of a school choral group who have worked hard all term to produce a show based on Christmas music from around the world. They have learnt complicated songs in unfamiliar languages and performed them at the end of term to a jam packed school hall full of parents, teachers and friends.

To mark their achievements, Nia takes some of the sheet music they have used, laminates it and cuts it into strips, labels it with the event's name and date, and then adds a tassel to make a bookmark. The next term she hands these out to all the performers and crew at a lunch she has organised to reflect on and celebrate the event.

DOI: 10.4324/9781003221296-33

How does this strategy maximise learning?

- *A souvenir* provides a reminder of the learning from an activity in the participant's day-to-day life.
- The presentation of a *Souvenir* provides a neat way to provide a highlight at the end of an activity.
- This strategy creates a natural opportunity to review and celebrate success when it is presented.

Pitfalls

- It can be costly both in terms of money and time to provide *Souvenirs*.
- The participants need to see the value in the *Souvenirs*, and they need to be useful or aesthetic, or they might be viewed as gimmicks and simply thrown away.
- If the exercise hasn't gone to plan, it might no longer be right to celebrate it with a *Souvenir*, even if you have spent time creating them.

If you are looking at this you might like to consider...

- Instruction Manual
- The Bigger Picture

Storyteller

Use a story to explain the rules and give a purpose to an activity

Use this strategy to...

Encourage Your Participants to Solve Problems	Motivate Your Participants

Storytelling has played a part in learning and education throughout history. By stepping into a fictional world, we can remove some of the barriers placed by reality and impose our own.

Inventing a story to explain why participants are doing an activity and why any 'arbitrary' rules are in place can help them engage with the task. If your team can imagine themselves 'crossing a swamp' on planks, even if they are on a patch of grass, it makes more sense why they shouldn't fall off.

The story that you tell must be simple enough to be readily understood, and any rules you impose must make sense within the story. By working in a slightly fictionalised version of your activity, you can apply limitations beyond those that naturally exist. A story can make rules seem less arbitrary and avoid setting you up against your group when you impose them.

A story can also be used to make theoretical problems more accessible. If participants can visualise the task they are trying to solve, they are more likely to be able to solve it and will have clearer language to discuss it with others.

By being a *Storyteller*, you can make an activity fun and engaging, especially for younger groups, and it provides them with a reason to do the activity and remember it afterwards.

Remember, however, that you are asking for your participants' goodwill in 'believing' your story. Make it too complicated or long winded and the learning that you hope they will get may be lost. Make sure that you don't get so enthusiastic about your story that you cannot bring the participants back to the learning.

The strategy in action

Isabelle teaches a science class to 14 year olds. They are looking at the topic of electricity, and rather than just give them the task of building an electrical generator, she decides to tell them a story to understand how their knowledge can be applied to a real-world problem.

She presents them with a portable fridge that can be used to store vaccines that are being distributed around sub-Saharan Africa. The fridge runs from a battery that needs regular charging.

She gives them various materials such as wood, cloth, glue, nails and screws, along with a small generator. Their challenge is to build a wind turbine that will keep the fridge charged while in remote locations.

The students can immediately see the purpose of the activity and why their knowledge is useful, and they have a clear goal as they start to apply that knowledge to Isabelle's challenge.

DOI: 10.4324/9781003221296-34

How does this strategy maximise learning?

- By being a *Storyteller*, you can use the fiction you create to impose arbitrary rules on activity that only make sense within the story.
- By using a story carefully, you can make an activity more accessible, more memorable, easier to visualise and provide participants with a common language to talk about it.
- It is fun, especially for younger groups, to participate in an activity with a story they are likely to engage with through their imagination.

Pitfalls

- Some participants will struggle to engage with a fictional story and will find it silly or childish.
- Your story will set the tone for the activity. A light-hearted or 'silly' story will set a light-hearted tone, which may distract from serious learning objectives.
- Not every activity needs a story. If you try to layer a story over an activity that obviously provides learning in its own right, you risk the participants feeling the story is a distraction.

If you are looking at this you might like to consider...

- Free Rein
- Mysterious Voice
- The Bigger Picture
- Written Brief

Sum of the Whole

Assign each member of the group a distinct part to play in achieving the goal

Use this strategy to...

Help Your Participants Plan and Organise	Help Your Participants See the Big Picture	Make Your Participants Think about Each Other and Their Differences	Ensure Your Participants Support Each Other

Providing participants with opportunities to take responsibility for specific parts of an activity can lead to powerful learning for them, helping them understand that their small contribution can combine with others' to achieve a goal. It can demonstrate to them that the *Sum of the Whole* is often greater than the parts individually.

Assigning areas of responsibility or allowing participants to choose their own can help engage participants in an activity. It can ensure that their individual actions have an impact on the outcome, and allows them a sense of pride in the team's achievement.

Areas of responsibility could be directly related to the task, or could have a wider focus, such as timekeeping, morale, record-keeping, getting feedback or liaising with you.

Even activities that naturally require distinct roles for participants to ensure success can benefit from a second level of areas of responsibility, so participants have to think about more than just the task in front of them.

If you have participants of varying ability, by assigning more challenging roles to the more able, you can provide differing levels of challenge within the same activity.

The strategy in action

Tom leads a school jazz band that are putting on a performance for parents. He is aware that for previous concerts students have simply turned up to rehearse and then play. The setting up and running of the event is normally left to staff. Tom feels that in some of the recent concerts the playing has lacked enthusiasm, and he decides that he wants his students to feel more ownership of their performances.

This time, in addition to learning the music, students are given other roles, such as creating programmes, laying out and dressing the stage, deciding on the dress-code, marketing the event, selling tickets and managing the budget.

As the date approaches, the students are more engaged than previously, they talk a lot about how their area of responsibility is going and there is a real buzz about 'their' concert. They practice harder than before, and the atmosphere on the night is lively and enthusiastic, which shows in the music.

DOI: 10.4324/9781003221296-35

How does this strategy maximise learning?

- Having an individual role for each participant can engage and provide a sense of responsibility.
- Allows participants of differing abilities to find challenge in the same activity.
- Helps participants to value and appreciate the roles played by others in their own successes.

Pitfalls

- ⚠ If roles are not created carefully, there can be a difference in the perception of status within a group, leading to conflict.
- ⚠ Any roles created must not feel trivial, otherwise participants will disengage from them and possibly the activity.
- ⚠ It is possible to overload a participant who already finds an activity challenging by giving them additional responsibilities.

If you are looking at this you might like to consider...

- Delegate
- Hidden Agendas
- Secret Agent

The Bigger Picture

Create a storyline that connects a lot of little tasks into something bigger

Use this strategy to...

Motivate Your Participants	Brief Your Participants Differently	Help Your Participants See the Big Picture	Help Your Participants Plan and Organise

If you have a number of activities to offer your participants, it can be a powerful learning experience to link them together into a *Bigger Picture*. A story or greater goal above that of the individual activities can help participants engage and provide a driver for them to tackle each part.

The story could be fiction or you could choose a real-world goal that your activities lead towards. If you are happy to weave a story around your activities, the choices are endless. Perhaps your participants are secret agents, hunting for treasure or looking for a missing person. If you'd rather something less fanciful, perhaps they earn points during the activities, write a guidebook to the activities or collect pieces of a jigsaw to assemble.

Don't expect participants to play characters; they must tackle the activities as themselves, not through roleplay. It is okay for them to pretend to be on a Moon mission, it's not okay for them to pretend to be Neil Armstrong.

Although time consuming to create, programmes with a *Bigger Picture* can be a lot of fun, and they engage participants' imagination, motivating and inspiring them. They are also useful as a way to provide continuity if your programme has long breaks in it, for example: 'When we left off, we had just discovered the location of...'.

They require care in their design, and there needs to be a balance of creativity and realism to stop them feeling silly. If you can sell your participants on a big 'story', you can often make smaller activities feel more meaningful than if they were run in isolation, as succeeding at them contributes to *The Bigger Picture*. Participants must also understand the 'real' reason for the activity; don't let them get so wrapped up in the story that they forget that they are supposed to be learning something.

The strategy in action

Phil runs a youth organisation for young people between the ages of 8 and 12 that meets weekly.

He wants them to undertake a number of tasks that will involve them working together, solving problems and overcoming challenges. He creates a story that links the tasks together, to provide continuity from week to week and to ensure they have fun.

The story is that a dinosaur skeleton has been stolen from a local museum, and their job is to return it. The skeleton has been split into its bones, and completion of each task will reveal the location of one of the bones. After they have successfully completed ten tasks, they will have all the bones and can reassemble them to the complete dinosaur. He themes the resources, briefings and tasks around archaeology and dinosaurs to help reinforce the story.

Each week the young people arrive at their meeting excited to track down the next bone. After they have collected all of them, Phil helps them reflect on how they had to work together, solve problems and overcome challenges to succeed.

DOI: 10.4324/9781003221296-36

How does this strategy maximise learning?

- Having a *Bigger Picture* is a good way of engaging your participants, can inspire them to achieve more and provides a 'flow' between activities.
- A *Bigger Picture* can be used to reduce the formality, making participants more relaxed and more receptive to learning.
- When participants succeed at their *Bigger Picture* goal, the experience is more memorable, allowing better recall of their learning.

Pitfalls

- The *Bigger Picture* is a driver for the learning experience, not the end result. It is easy to get lost in your own creativity.
- If each part of the *Bigger Picture* needs to be completed in order to meet your ultimate goal, it is important to have contingencies in place if the participants fail a section.
- Members of the public won't understand *The Bigger Picture* that you and your participants have access to. Beware of unexpected reactions from them!

If you are looking at this you might like to consider...

- Instruction Manual
- Iterative Goals
- Souvenir
- Storyteller

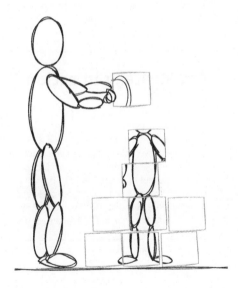

Train Tracks

Create a precise plan for the group to follow

Use this strategy to...

Make It Likely Your Participants Will Succeed	Build Participants' Confidence

Sometimes you want to know exactly how an activity will play out and there isn't much room for deviation. This is especially true in situations where the consequences of failure outweigh the learning the participants would get from having more freedom. These consequences might include safety, financial, time, interpersonal, environmental issues or impact on future activities.

By laying *Train Tracks* for your participants to follow in the form of a clear, comprehensive plan and an insistence that they follow that plan, they can undertake an activity that might otherwise be too complicated, challenging or hazardous.

You must be on hand throughout the activity to both monitor the group's adherence to the plan and to deal with any situations that the plan does not cover.

When using this strategy, you must have decided that the benefits for the participants of taking on the challenge outweigh the lack of control they have and the possible reduction in learning this brings. It can also be used during the first attempt of an activity, with more control being handed to the group as they get more experienced.

The strategy in action

Alan is introducing a group of engineering apprentices to Non-Destructive Testing, where radiation is used to look for faults in welding.

The apprentices have never used a radiation source before, so after explaining the hazards involved, Alan lays out a very clear plan for them to follow, which he writes on the whiteboard. The apprentices follow the plan step-by-step, and Alan is on hand to monitor their actions, correct any deviations from the plan and answer any questions not covered by it.

Once the radiation sources are safely back in their storage, he reviews the process with the apprentices and lets them know that next time, they will be making their own plan, which he will approve before they follow it (using the *Drag and Drop* approach).

DOI: 10.4324/9781003221296-37

How does this strategy maximise learning?

- Laying *Train Tracks* is a good way to help maximise your participants' chance of success.
- By having a prepared and clear plan, groups can achieve more than they could if left to their own devices.
- Using this strategy you can allow participants to negotiate safety, financial, time, interpersonal or environmental issues that otherwise might be too challenging.

Pitfalls

- This strategy offers little opportunity for the participants to provide input and so their learning must come from the experience itself, rather than the planning and running of it.
- Capable groups might find following *Train Tracks* boring or childish and disengage from the activity.
- Your plan that you create must be clear, easy to follow and likely to result in success, or your participants may lose trust in you if they fail.

If you are looking at this you might like to consider...

- Drag and Drop
- Leg Up
- Pulling Strings
- Wind Up and Let Go

Wind Up and Let Go

Provide a lot of praise and enthusiasm before the activity to give the group confidence

Use this strategy to...

Build Participants' Confidence	Motivate Your Participants

Sometimes participants lack confidence in themselves, but you are confident in their ability to achieve. To get them to take their first step, often all that is needed is to fire them up with lots of enthusiasm, praise and evidence of your confidence in them.

By infusing participants with your confidence and enthusiasm, you help them to believe they can take on the challenge ahead of them and that they are ready to go. Once they start, you can step back and let them get on with it.

Your support before they start could be in the form of being a *Cheerleader*, providing plenty of enthusiasm, or it might be a reminder of how much they have achieved to get to that point. In some cases, a quiet acknowledgement of worry and steadying of nerves, might be appropriate, or some piece of last minute wisdom.

Your goal is to inhibit and overwhelm any doubt that is forming in your participants' mind, and to ensure that they believe that they tackle what's ahead, or at least that it is worth starting!

The strategy in action

Neil is leading a group of young skiers on a trip. After a couple of days of practice, they are comfortable on the easier slopes.

As a challenge, they board the lift to the top of the mountain, where a famous piste leads all the way to the bottom. The top in particular feels steep and intimidating, with high peaks surrounding a steep bowl.

Neil is confident that all in his group have the skills to tackle the descent, but understandably some are nervous. As they get ready and on the way up, Neil is unrelentingly enthusiastic and fills them with praise, while reminding them of a few key basics to focus on.

By the time they are at the top, Neil hasn't given them any time to develop nervous thoughts, and he continues to enthuse and excite them as they get ready, ensuring they set off enthusiastically to tackle such a famous challenge. As they depart, he keeps his distance and with a watchful eye, proudly observing them making the descent and making decisions for themselves.

DOI: 10.4324/9781003221296-38

How does this strategy maximise learning?

♀ *Wind Up and Let Go* ensures that your participants at least start their activity with a belief that success is possible.
♀ This strategy is a good 'stepping stone' between being involved with your group throughout an activity and letting them operate entirely independently.
♀ Timed at a critical moment, a very small interaction with participants has the potential to change their mindset towards the possibility of success.

Pitfalls

⚠ To use this strategy, you must be confident that your participants can achieve the challenge they are taking on, otherwise your credibility and their self-confidence will be dented.
⚠ If you haven't yet earned their trust, your enthusiasm and praise may feel hollow or empty to an under confident group.
⚠ If your participants are more nervous or less confident then you realise, *Wind Up and Let Go* can make them feel like you aren't taking their worries seriously enough, damaging their trust in you.

If you are looking at this you might like to consider...

🔭 Charge
🔭 Cheerleader
🔭 Islands of Safety
🔭 Train Tracks

Written Brief

Hand out written instructions to the group with all the information needed and leave the participants to follow them

Use this strategy to...

Brief Your Participants Differently	Empower Your Participants	Get Your Participants to Think for Themselves

In this strategy, you create a full set of instructions for the activity before it happens. When you come to run the activity, the group is simply given the brief and you stand back and let them get on with it.

Your written brief might include how to set up the activity, do the activity, safety information, top tips and the specific areas that will be reviewed. Include all information you think the group might need, but try to keep it as concise as possible. You should discourage participants from asking you lots of questions, because many can be answered with the phrase 'It's all in the brief'.

If you have written the instructions well enough, the group should be able to attempt to complete the task without further interference from you. The first few times you use a brief, you can make yourself available to clarify details, it is possible that you have missed a detail or two, but if your instructions are clear enough, you should find yourself just observing.

This strategy is time consuming to set up but it can be especially valuable when a task is going to be used lots of times and allows different groups to have a similar experience, even if the activity is run by different people.

The strategy in action

Kala is teaching a class of 10 year olds how to test for the presence of starch in food using iodine solution. She creates a written brief, which starts with a list of equipment, then some safety information, then a list of instructions to follow to carry out the experiment, and finishes with some questions the students should discuss with their lab partners.

She gives the document to a colleague to work their way though and receives some suggested changes she could make to clarify the instructions.

During the lesson, she hands out the brief, along with trays of equipment and the students follow the instructions at their own pace, including tidying up. She then steps back completely, and apart from monitoring their safety, allows them to solve their own problems as they arise. She enjoys the opportunity to observe her students' behaviours as they are working. At the end, she gathers the students' answers to the questions onto the board and they discuss them as a class.

DOI: 10.4324/9781003221296-39

How does this strategy maximise learning?

- This strategy is really empowering for the group because they are in control of their exercise.
- It stops an 'us against them' situation developing, where the group feel they are being pitted against any changing instructions of the person running the activity.
- *Written Brief* allows you to stay neutral, which means you can potentially be more challenging in a review, because you were less involved in the exercise.
- It forces you to think through the activity very carefully beforehand to write your instructions.
- The instructions can be kept with the equipment needed, making it very quick and simple to run tasks. This also allows you to run multiple exercises at the same time.

Pitfalls

- There isn't much flexibility in this strategy; you can't adjust the brief during the activity to better suit the group or time available.
- The brief must be clear and unambiguous. If the group need to ask lots of questions, the self-sufficiency this strategy encourages will be lost.
- Writing good, clear instructions ahead of their use is challenging and time consuming.

If you are looking at this you might like to consider...

- In the Picture
- Listen Very Carefully
- Mime Artist
- Mysterious Voice

Wizard

Inspire the group with expert skills beyond their comprehension

Use this strategy to...

Inspire Your Participants	Help Your Participants See the Big Picture

In this strategy, your aim is to inspire the group to improve their skills at an activity by showing them what is possible when they become competent. To make it work, you must be effortlessly competent in the activity you are running, and you should be able to do things that the group didn't even know were possible.

Pick something that you think will inspire them and demonstrate it. You should perform it flawlessly and without ceremony. Whatever you chose, it should be something that the group didn't know was possible. As such, it should appear like you have just performed magic.

This isn't a chance for you to show off, it's not about leaving them in awe of you. It's about leaving them excited by what is possible as they improve.

It is important that you make it clear that you don't expect them to be able to do the same yet, although if safe and sensible to do so, there might be no harm in letting them have a go.

When this strategy works, the participants should be gobsmacked and left in awe of what an expert can do. The desired outcome is that they head off to their own practice inspired by having seen what they might be able to achieve one day!

The strategy in action

Katy is teaching tennis. She is working with her players on their return of the ball.

The players are improving slowly, but they are starting to flag and engagement is dropping. Suddenly Katy turns away from the oncoming ball and plays a perfect return straight between her legs that catches the players off their guard, scores a point and makes them gasp.

The players' imagination is sparked and suddenly they are trying to repeat her trick, and the practice session has lots more energy. They don't have much success but it has lifted their spirits and given them something to aspire to.

DOI: 10.4324/9781003221296-40

How does this strategy maximise learning?

- This strategy provides inspiration and a little 'magic' to help the group realise how exciting the activity they are doing is, and what is possible if they persevere.
- If a group thinks they know it all, *Wizard* can remind the group they have a lot to learn.
- If a group's interest in an activity is flagging, this strategy can help inspire and rekindle their interest.
- Being a *Wizard* can bring the 'magic' of an activity right before a group's eyes, which might inspire them to find out more.

Pitfalls

- *Wizard* can demoralise your group, as you show them how far away they are from your level.
- This strategy can also trivialise skills that have taken years to master. When your group sees you making it look easy, they might feel silly or get frustrated with their own progress.
- There is a risk that you make this about you and your skills, not your group and their development, and you just look like you are showing off.

If you are looking at this you might like to consider...

- Peer Expert
- Saviour

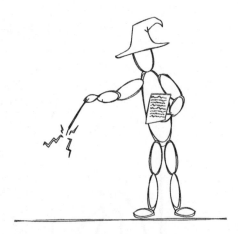

Let's Carry on the Conversation

Both the authors are passionate about developing people through learning experiences whether they be in the classroom, on the sports field, up a mountain, on the sea or on the stage.

We love discovering what others are up to and providing support where we can use our expertise to design and develop really great experiences for learners, or where we can help others do the same.

If you are interested in continuing the conversation about learning through experience, do not hesitate to get in touch.

amplifyingactivities@gmail.com

DOI: 10.4324/9781003221296-41